Better Homes and Gardens®

CHRISTMAS COOKING
FROM THE HEART™

A Warm Welcome

Meredith® Consumer Marketing
Des Moines, Iowa

CHRISTMAS COOKING
FROM THE HEART™

MEREDITH CORPORATION CONSUMER MARKETING
Vice President, Consumer Marketing: Janet Donnelly
Consumer Marketing Product Director: Heather Sorensen
Consumer Marketing Product Manager: Janece Schwartzkopf
Business Director: Ron Clingman
Senior Production Manager: Al Rodruck
Photographers: Marty Baldwin, Kritsada Panichgul

WATERBURY PUBLICATIONS, INC.
Editorial Director: Lisa Kingsley
Creative Director: Ken Carlson
Associate Editors: Tricia Bergman, Mary Williams
Associate Design Director: Doug Samuelson
Graphic Designer: Mindy Samuelson
Contributing Copy Editor: Terri Fredrickson
Contributing Proofreader: Gretchen Kauffman
Contributing Indexer: Elizabeth T. Parson
Contributing Food Stylists: Annie Peterson, Jennifer Peterson,
Charles Worthington

BETTER HOMES AND GARDENS® MAGAZINE
Editor in Chief: Gayle Goodson Butler
Art Director: Michael D. Belknap
Senior Deputy Editor: Nancy Wall Hopkins
Editorial Assistant: Renee Irey

MEREDITH PUBLISHING GROUP
President: Tom Harty

MEREDITH CORPORATION
Chairman and Chief Executive Officer: Stephen M. Lacy

In Memoriam: E.T. Meredith III (1933–2003)

Test Kitchen

Our seal assures you that every recipe in *Christmas Cooking from the Heart*™ has been tested in the Better Homes and Gardens® Test Kitchen. This means that each recipe is practical and reliable, and meets our high standards of taste appeal. We guarantee your satisfaction with this book for as long as you own it.

All of us at Meredith® Consumer Marketing are dedicated to providing you with information and ideas to enhance your home. We welcome your comments and suggestions. Write to us at: Meredith Consumer Marketing, 1716 Locust St., Des Moines, IA 50309-3023. *Christmas Cooking from the Heart*™ is available by mail. To order editions from past years, call 800/627-5490.

Cover Photography:
Front cover: Carrot-Coconut Cream Cake with Rum-Raisin Filling (page 76)

JUMBO
MARSHMALLOW
TREATS, PAGE 127

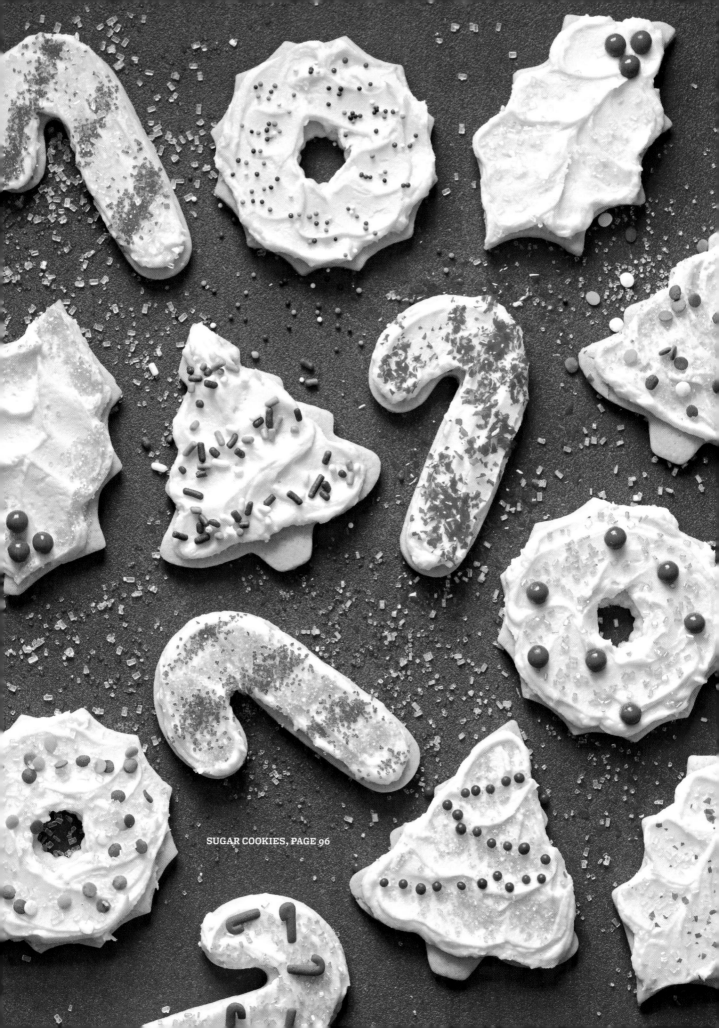

SUGAR COOKIES, PAGE 96

Table of Contents

A Warm Welcome

FROM HEART AND HANDS There is perhaps no better way to show the important people in your life how you feel about them than to cook or bake something wonderful and share it with them. Especially during the holiday season, the gift of time spent in the kitchen and the end result—whether it's a lavish Christmas Eve spread served to close family or a beautifully wrapped box of homemade cookies or candy for your child's teacher—is meaningful and much appreciated. *Better Homes and Gardens® Christmas Cooking from the Heart* can help you create a very special holiday season for family and friends this year. It's full of fresh takes on familiar foods for a festive family feast (see Lemon-Thyme Split-Roasted Turkey, page 12), savory small bites for nibbling and mingling (see Crab Rangoon Strudel, page 35), and more indulgent desserts than you can tempt guests with in one holiday season (see Bread Pudding with Cinnamon-Pecan Syrup, page 88, and chocolate-cloaked Almond Cheesecake, page 86). Time spent with family and friends enjoying food and fellowship is the greatest gift of the season. Happy Holidays!

CHOCOLATE-ESPRESSO
CHIFFON CAKE, PAGE 78

SUNDAY BEEF RIB
ROAST, PAGE 12

Sit-Down Dinner

PULL UP A CHAIR Formal but not fussy, these dishes make a meal a special event. A beautiful rib roast, herb-roasted turkey, a glazed, spiral-sliced ham—and an array of elegant sides—draw friends and family to the table for food and connection.

APRICOT-STUFFED PORK
TENDERLOIN

Apricot-Stuffed Pork Tenderloin

PREP 45 minutes
ROAST 50 minutes at 375°F
STAND 15 minutes
MAKES 12 servings

4 slices white bread, torn
3 tablespoons butter, melted
  Nonstick cooking spray
1 cup dried apricots
½ cup fresh parsley leaves
2 teaspoons fresh thyme leaves
½ cup chopped onion (1 medium)
½ cup chopped celery (1 stalk)
2 tablespoons olive oil
½ cup chicken broth
½ teaspoon salt
¼ teaspoon black pepper
2 1- to 1½-pound pork tenderloins
½ cup apricot preserves, melted

1. Preheat oven to 375°F. Line a 15×10×1-inch baking pan with foil; set aside. For stuffing, place bread in a food processor. Cover and process until coarse crumbs form. Transfer to a large bowl. Drizzle with melted butter; toss to coat.
2. Spread crumbs evenly in the prepared baking pan. Bake for 6 to 8 minutes or until golden, stirring once. Return bread crumbs to the large bowl. Place a rack in the foil-lined baking pan and coat with cooking spray; set pan aside.
3. In the food processor combine dried apricots, parsley, and thyme. Cover and process with on/off pulses until finely chopped. Stir mixture into bread crumbs.
4. In the food processor combine onion and celery. Cover and process until finely chopped. In a small skillet cook onion and celery in hot oil over medium heat about 5 minutes or until tender. Stir in broth; cook for 1 minute. Add onion mixture, ½ teaspoon salt, and ¼ teaspoon pepper to bread mixture, stirring to moisten.
5. Trim fat from meat. Using a sharp knife, make a lengthwise cut down the center of each tenderloin, cutting to, but not through, the opposite

side. Cut horizontally into the meat, slicing away from the center cut. Repeat on the opposite side. Place each tenderloin between two pieces of plastic wrap. Using the flat side of a meat mallet, pound lightly from center to edges into a 12×8-inch rectangle.

6. Spread stuffing over meat to within 1 inch of the edges. Starting from a short side, roll each rectangle into a spiral. Tie with 100%-cotton kitchen string. Place stuffed tenderloins, seam sides down, on the rack in the foil-lined baking pan. Sprinkle with additional salt and pepper.

7. Roast, uncovered, for 50 to 55 minutes or until an instant-read thermometer inserted in the stuffing registers 145°F, brushing meat with some of the preserves during the last 5 minutes of roasting. Remove from oven. Cover meat with foil; let stand for 15 minutes. Remove string from meat. Slice meat; serve with the remaining preserves.

PER SERVING *247 cal., 7 g fat (3 g sat. fat), 77 mg chol., 289 mg sodium, 21 g carb., 1 g fiber, 24 g pro.*

Baked Ham with Mustard-Plum Glaze

PREP **20 minutes**
BAKE **1 hour 45 minutes at 350°F**
STAND **10 minutes**
MAKES **12 servings**

- 1 **3- to 4-pound small bone-in ham**
- 1 **10-ounce jar plum jam (1 cup)**
- ¼ **cup pomegranate juice**
- ⅛ **teaspoon ground cloves (optional)**
- 1 **tablespoon Dijon mustard**
- 6 **medium leeks**
  Salt and black pepper
- ½ **cup finely shredded Parmesan cheese**
- ½ **cup soft bread crumbs**
- 2 **tablespoons butter, melted**
  Fresh sage leaves (optional)

1. Preheat oven to 350°F. Place ham on a rack in a foil-lined roasting pan. Bake, uncovered, for 45 minutes.

2. For the glaze, in a small saucepan stir together jam, pomegranate juice, and, if desired, ground cloves. Heat over low heat until melted and combined. Spoon half of the jam mixture over ham. Tent ham with foil. Bake for 1 to 1½ hours or until meat thermometer registers 140°F. Remove and let stand, covered, for 10 minutes. Stir mustard into remaining jam mixture; heat through.

3. For leeks, trim root ends and tough green ends. Halve leeks lengthwise. Remove and discard tough outer layers of leeks. Rinse well. Arrange leek halves in a 2-quart rectangular baking dish. Add 2 tablespoons water. Sprinkle leeks lightly with salt, pepper, and ¼ cup of the cheese. Cover with foil. Bake in the oven with the ham for 35 minutes. Uncover; sprinkle with bread crumbs and remaining cheese. Drizzle with melted butter. Bake, uncovered, for 15 minutes more or until leeks are tender and topping is brown.

4. To serve, spoon some of the remaining mustard-plum glaze over the ham. Slice ham and serve with remaining mustard-plum glaze and leeks. If desired, garnish with sage leaves.

PER SERVING *310 cal., 13 g fat (5 g sat. fat), 69 mg chol., 1,001 mg sodium, 25 g carb., 1 g fiber, 24 g pro.*

BAKED HAM WITH MUSTARD-PLUM GLAZE

Sunday Beef Rib Roast

PREP **30 minutes**
ROAST **1 hour 45 minutes at 350°F**
STAND **15 minutes**
MAKES **10 servings**

- 1 4- to 5-pound beef rib roast (chin bone removed)
- 1 teaspoon cracked black peppercorns
- ½ teaspoon salt
- 1 pound baby carrots with tops, trimmed
- 1 pound small red skinned potatoes (halve any larger potatoes)
- 1 15-ounce can butter beans, rinsed and drained
- 3 to 4 cups baby spinach

1. Preheat oven to 350°F. Sprinkle beef roast with cracked pepper, salt, and half of the Bacon Topping. Place meat, bone side down, in a shallow roasting pan. Insert an oven-going meat thermometer into center of roast.
2. Roast, uncovered, for 45 minutes. Arrange carrots and potatoes around roast. Stir gently to coat vegetables with any cooking liquid. Roast 1 to 1¼ hours more or until meat thermometer registers 135°F for medium-rare. Sprinkle meat with remaining half of Bacon Topping; cover and let stand for 15 minutes. Temperature of meat after standing should be 145°F. (For medium, roast for 2¼ to 2¾ hours or until meat thermometer registers 150°F. Cover with foil; let stand for 15 minutes. Temperature after standing should be 160°F.) Push meat and carrots and potatoes to one side of pan. Stir beans and spinach into drippings in other side of pan. Top with reserved bacon pieces.

Bacon Topping Cook 4 slices of bacon until crisp; drain on paper towels. Chop half of the bacon; stir in 1 tablespoon chopped fresh thyme and 1½ teaspoons chopped fresh rosemary. Break remaining half of the bacon into large pieces to sprinkle on spinach mixture. Store in refrigerator until needed.

Tip For added garlic flavor, cut 3 garlic cloves into slivers. Before roasting, cut shallow slits all over meat; insert garlic slivers into slits. Roast as directed.

PER SERVING 492 cal., 32 g fat (13 g sat. fat), 91 mg chol., 468 mg sodium, 19 g carb., 4 g fiber, 32 g pro.

Lemon-Thyme Split-Roasted Turkey

PREP **30 minutes**
ROAST **1 hour 30 minutes at 375°F**
STAND **15 minutes**
MAKES **12 servings**

- 2 medium onions, cut into wedges
- 2 lemons, cut into quarters
- 1 stalk celery, cut into 2-inch pieces
- 4 fresh thyme sprigs
- 8 cloves garlic
- ½ cup butter, softened
- ¼ cup snipped fresh thyme
- 2 teaspoons finely shredded lemon peel
- 2 tablespoons lemon juice
- 2 tablespoons finely chopped shallot (1 medium)
- 1 tablespoon vegetable oil
- ½ teaspoon kosher salt
- ½ teaspoon freshly ground black pepper
- 1 8- to 10-pound fresh or frozen turkey, thawed if frozen

1. Position the oven rack in the bottom third of the oven. Preheat oven to 375°F. In a large roasting pan combine onions, lemons, celery, thyme sprigs, and garlic; set aside.
2. In a medium bowl combine butter, snipped thyme, lemon peel, lemon juice, shallot, oil, salt, and pepper; set aside.
3. Remove neck and giblets from turkey; discard. Rinse the turkey cavity body; pat dry with paper towels. Place turkey, breast side down, on a cutting board. Using kitchen shears, make a lengthwise cut down one side of the backbone, starting from the neck end. Repeat on the other side of the backbone. Remove and discard backbone. Turn turkey, cut side down. Flatten turkey as much as possible with your hands. Cut off and discard tips of wings. Using kitchen shears or a large sharp knife, carefully cut through the entire breastbone, creating two equal halves.
4. Rub herb-butter mixture over turkey on all sides, massaging some of the mixture underneath the skin. Place turkey halves, skin sides up, on top of vegetables in roasting pan. Insert an oven-going meat thermometer into the center of an inside thigh muscle. The thermometer should not touch bone.
5. Roast, uncovered, for 1½ to 2 hours or until meat thermometer registers 175°F. (The juices should run clear and drumsticks should move easily in their sockets.) Remove from oven. Cover turkey halves with foil; let stand for 15 minutes before carving. Discard vegetables in roasting pan.

PER SERVING 547 cal., 30 g fat (12 g sat. fat), 207 mg chol., 821 mg sodium, 5 g carb., 1 g fiber, 57 g pro.

SUNDAY BEEF RIB ROAST

LEMON-THYME SPLIT-ROASTED TURKEY

FRESH CRANBERRY-CITRUS RELISH

1. Combine all ingredients in a nonreactive medium-size saucepan. Bring to simmering. Cover partially and simmer very slowly for 40 minutes. Uncover and simmer for 10 minutes longer or until the fruit is tender and the port is slightly reduced and thickened. Remove and discard bay leaves.

PER SERVING *201 cal., 0 g fat, 0 g chol., 49 mg sodium, 37 g carb., 3 g fiber, 1 g pro.*

Vidalia Onion and Maple Conserve

PREP **30 minutes** COOK **30 minutes**
PROCESS **5 minutes**
MAKES **7 servings**

- ¼ cup butter
- ¼ cup olive oil
- 2½ pounds Vidalia onions or other sweet onions (such as Walla Walla or Maui), quartered and thinly sliced (8 cups)
- 2 teaspoons sea salt
- 2 tablespoons fresh thyme leaves
- 1 teaspoon freshly ground black pepper
- 1 cup pure maple syrup
- ¼ cup sherry vinegar

1. In an extra-large skillet heat butter and oil over medium-high heat until butter melts. Add onions and salt. Cook about 5 minutes or until onions start to soften, stirring frequently. Reduce heat to medium-low. Stir in thyme and pepper. Cover and cook for 10 to 12 minutes or until onions are very tender, stirring twice.
2. Increase heat to medium-high. Add maple syrup. Bring just to boiling. Reduce heat to medium. Cook, uncovered, for 15 to 20 minutes or until most of the liquid has evaporated, stirring frequently. Remove from heat; stir in vinegar.

PER SERVING *109 cal., 5 g fat (2 g sat. fat), 6 mg chol., 180 mg sodium, 16 g carb., 1 g fiber, 1 g pro.*

Fresh Cranberry-Citrus Relish

PREP **20 minutes**
STAND **30 minutes**
MAKES **10 servings**

- 1 medium seedless orange
- 1 medium lemon
- 1 medium apple
- ½ cup sugar
- 4 cups fresh or frozen cranberries

1. Finely shred the peel from orange and lemon. Remove the remaining peel with a sharp knife and discard. Cut orange and lemon into wedges; discard any seeds. Core apple and cut into chunks.
2. Place fruit and peel in a food processor. Add sugar. Cover and process with several on/off turns until coarsely chopped. Add cranberries.

Cover and process with on/off turns until chopped. Transfer mixture to a medium bowl.
3. Cover and let stand at room temperature for 30 to 45 minutes before serving, stirring occasionally.

PER SERVING *77 cal., 0 g fat, 0 g chol., 1 mg sodium, 21 g carb., 3 g fiber, 0 g pro.*

Plum Compote

PREP **10 minutes** COOK **50 minutes**
MAKES **12 servings**

- 1 cup pitted prunes
- 1 cup dried apricots
- ¾ cup dried apple slices, halved
- ½ cup dried cherries
- 3 fresh bay leaves or 1 dried bay leaf
- ¼ cup granulated sugar
- ¼ teaspoon kosher salt
- 3 cups port wine or cranberry juice

CORN BREAD STUFFING WITH
TOMATOES AND SAGE

Corn Bread Stuffing with Tomatoes and Sausage

PREP **30 minutes**
BAKE **55 minutes at 325°F**
MAKES **10 servings**

12 cups 1-inch corn bread cubes
 1 pound bulk hot Italian sausage
 4 cups chopped onions (4 large)
 3 cloves garlic, minced
 ½ cup dry white wine or chicken broth
 1 cup dried tomatoes (not oil-packed), chopped
 ¼ cup finely snipped fresh sage
 ¼ cup finely snipped fresh parsley
 1 teaspoon kosher salt
 1 14.5-ounce can diced tomatoes, drained
1½ cups chicken broth
 2 tablespoons butter, cut up

1. Preheat oven to 325°F. Spread corn bread cubes in two 15×10×1-inch baking pans. Bake for 10 to 15 minutes or until lightly toasted, stirring once; cool.
2. Meanwhile, in a large skillet cook sausage, onions, and garlic over medium-high heat until sausage is brown, using a wooden spoon to break up meat as it cooks. Drain off fat. Carefully add wine, stirring to scrape up any crusty brown bits. Stir in dried tomatoes, sage, parsley, and salt. Remove from heat; let stand for 5 minutes.

3. In an extra-large bowl combine corn bread cubes, sausage mixture, and diced tomatoes. Drizzle corn bread mixture with broth, tossing gently to moisten. Transfer mixture to a large cast-iron skillet or 3-quart rectangular baking dish. Dot with butter.
4. Bake, covered, for 30 minutes. Bake, uncovered, for 15 to 20 minutes more or until heated through.
Tip For a milder version, use bulk pork sausage in place of the hot Italian sausage.
PER SERVING *479 cal., 23 g fat (8 g sat. fat), 77 mg chol., 1,343 mg sodium, 52 g carb., 5 g fiber, 15 g pro.*

Risotto is a special-occasion dish. It takes a little standing and stirring, but the creamy, indulgent result is well worth the effort.

RISOTTO WITH CARAMELIZED ONIONS, BACON, AND MUSHROOMS

Risotto with Caramelized Onions, Bacon, and Mushrooms

PREP 30 minutes COOK 25 minutes
MAKES 6 servings

- 2 tablespoons olive oil
- 1 cup chopped onion (1 large)
- 4 slices bacon, chopped
- 6 ounces fresh cremini mushrooms or assorted fresh mushrooms, thinly sliced (2⅓ cups)
  Salt
- ⅔ cup dry Marsala
- 1½ cups arborio rice
- 5 cups homemade chicken stock or reduced-sodium chicken broth
- ½ cup freshly grated Parmigiano-Reggiano cheese
- 2 tablespoons unsalted butter
  Cracked black pepper
  Grated Parmesan cheese (optional)

1. In a large deep skillet heat oil over medium-low heat. Add onion and bacon; cook about 6 minutes or until onion is tender and bacon just begins to crisp. Stir in mushrooms and ¼ teaspoon salt; cook about 5 minutes or until mushrooms are tender, stirring occasionally. Carefully stir in ⅓ cup of the Marsala. Cook and stir about 3 minutes or until liquid is absorbed. Stir in rice. Cook and stir over medium heat for 2 to 3 minutes or until rice begins to brown. Stir in the remaining ⅓ cup Marsala. Cook and stir until liquid is absorbed.
2. Meanwhile, in a large saucepan bring chicken stock to boiling; reduce heat and simmer. Slowly add ½ cup of the hot stock to the rice mixture, stirring constantly. Continue to cook and stir over medium heat until liquid is absorbed. Add another ½ cup of the hot stock to the rice mixture, stirring constantly. Continue to cook and stir until the liquid is absorbed. Add the remaining hot stock, ½ cup at a time, stirring constantly until the broth has been absorbed. (This should take 25 to 30 minutes total.)

WILD RICE
DRESSING

3. Stir in cheese and butter. Season to taste with pepper. If desired, sprinkle with grated Parmesan cheese.
PER SERVING *524 cal., 27 g fat (11 g sat. fat), 48 mg chol., 1,311 mg sodium, 43 g carb., 1 g fiber, 20 g pro.*

Wild Rice Dressing

PREP 20 minutes COOK 40 minutes
MAKES 6 servings

- ½ cup uncooked wild rice
- 1 14.5-ounce can reduced-sodium chicken broth
- ½ cup dry white wine or chicken broth
- ½ cup uncooked white or brown rice
- ½ teaspoon poultry seasoning
- 2 cups sliced fresh mushrooms, such as cremini, shiitake, and/or button
- 1 cup chopped carrots (2 medium)
- ¾ cup thinly sliced green onions (6)
- ½ cup chopped red sweet pepper (1 small)
- 2 tablespoons butter
- ¾ cup pine nuts, toasted (see tip, page 25)
- ⅓ cup finely shredded Parmesan cheese
- ¼ teaspoon salt
- ¼ teaspoon black pepper

1. Rinse uncooked wild rice in a strainer under cold water for 1 minute; drain. In a large saucepan combine wild rice, broth, wine, uncooked brown rice (if using), and poultry seasoning. Bring to boiling; reduce heat. Simmer, covered, for 40 minutes or until rice is tender. If using, add white rice the last 20 minutes of cooking time. If necessary, drain any remaining liquid.
2. Meanwhile, in a large skillet cook mushrooms, carrots, onions, and sweet pepper in hot butter over medium heat for 5 to 8 minutes or until vegetables are tender. Stir in pine nuts, cheese, salt, and black pepper. Stir vegetable mixture into wild rice mixture.
PER SERVING *316 cal., 17 g fat (4 g sat. fat), 13 mg chol., 383 mg sodium, 30 g carb., 3 g fiber, 10 g pro.*

Rustic Garlic Mashed Potatoes

PREP 25 minutes
SLOW COOK 6 hours (low) or
3 hours (high)
MAKES 12 servings

- 3 pounds potatoes, peeled and cut into 2-inch pieces
- 6 cloves garlic, halved
- 1 bay leaf
- 2 14.5-ounce cans chicken broth with roasted garlic
- 1 cup whole milk
- ¼ cup butter
- 1 teaspoon salt
  Black pepper
  Fresh bay leaves (optional)

1. In a 3½- or 4-quart slow cooker combine potatoes, garlic, and 1 bay leaf. Pour broth over mixture in cooker.
2. Cover and cook on low-heat setting for 6 to 8 hours or on high-heat setting for 3 to 4 hours.
3. Drain potatoes in a colander set over a bowl to catch the cooking liquid; set liquid aside. Remove and discard bay leaf. Return potatoes to slow cooker. Using a potato masher, mash potatoes to desired consistency.
4. In a small saucepan heat milk and butter until milk is steaming and butter is almost melted. Add milk mixture and salt to mashed potatoes. Stir in enough of the reserved cooking liquid to make mashed potatoes light and fluffy.
5. Transfer mashed potatoes to a serving bowl. Sprinkle potatoes with pepper. If desired, garnish with fresh bay leaves.
To Make Ahead Prepare as directed, except leave mashed potatoes in slow cooker. Cover and keep warm on warm setting or low-heat setting for up to 2 hours. Reserve cooking liquid. If potatoes thicken, stir in enough of the reserved cooking liquid to make mashed potatoes light and fluffy. Serve as directed.
PER SERVING *135 cal., 5 g fat (3 g sat. fat), 13 mg chol., 496 mg sodium, 21 g carb., 1 g fiber, 3 g pro.*

RED LENTIL, QUINOA, AND FLAXSEED PILAF

Red Lentil, Quinoa, and Flaxseed Pilaf

PREP 15 minutes   COOK 28 minutes
STAND 5 minutes
MAKES 10 servings

- ⅔ cup dry red lentils
- ⅔ cup quinoa
- 2 tablespoons olive oil
- ⅔ cup finely chopped shallots or onion
- 4 cloves garlic, minced
- ¼ cup flaxseeds
- 2 14.5-ounce cans reduced-sodium chicken broth
- 2 cups chopped red or green sweet peppers (2 large)
- 2 teaspoons snipped fresh thyme or ½ teaspoon dried thyme, crushed
  Fresh thyme sprigs (optional)

1. Rinse and drain lentils and quinoa separately. In a large saucepan heat oil over medium heat. Add shallots and garlic; cook and stir for 3 minutes. Add quinoa and flaxseeds; cook and stir about 5 minutes or until quinoa is lightly browned.
2. Add lentils and chicken broth. Bring to boiling; reduce heat. Cover and simmer for 15 minutes. Stir in sweet peppers and snipped or dried thyme. Cover and cook about 5 minutes more or until quinoa and lentils are tender. Let stand, covered, for 5 minutes. If desired, garnish with thyme sprigs.
PER SERVING *152 cal., 5 g fat (1 g sat. fat), 0 mg chol., 198 mg sodium, 20 g carb., 4 g fiber, 7 g pro.*

CELERY ROOT, POTATO, AND PEAR MASH

Celery Root, Potato, and Pear Mash

PREP **15 minutes**
COOK **20 minutes** MAKES **6 servings**

- 8 ounces celery root, peeled and cut into 1½-inch pieces
- 1 pound russet potatoes, peeled and cut into 1½-inch pieces
- 2 cups peeled very ripe pears cut into 1½-inch pieces (2 medium)
- ½ cup whipping cream
- ¼ cup butter
  Salt
  Freshly ground black pepper
- 2 tablespoons snipped fresh parsley

1. In a large saucepan cook celery root, covered, in boiling lightly salted water for 5 minutes. Add potatoes. Cook, covered, for 20 to 25 minutes or until tender; drain. Return potato mixture to saucepan.

2. Meanwhile, in a small saucepan combine pears, whipping cream, and butter. Bring to boiling.* Remove from heat.

3. Mash potato mixture with a potato masher or an electric mixer on low until smooth. Season to taste with salt and pepper. Mash pear mixture with a potato masher or a fork until smooth. Stir pear mixture into potato mixture just until combined. Sprinkle with parsley.

*Tip If pears are firm, simmer in whipping cream for 5 to 10 minutes or until tender enough to mash.

PER SERVING *229 cal., 15 g fat (10 g sat. fat), 48 mg chol., 311 mg sodium, 23 g carb., 3 g fiber, 2 g pro.*

OVERNIGHT
REFRIGERATOR ROLLS

Overnight Refrigerator Rolls

PREP 35 minutes CHILL overnight
RISE 45 minutes
BAKE 12 minutes at 375°F
MAKES 24 servings

1¼ cups warm water (105°F to 115°F)
1 package active dry yeast
4 to 4¼ cups all-purpose flour
⅓ cup sugar
⅓ cup butter, melted, or vegetable oil
1 egg
1 teaspoon salt
Nonstick cooking spray
2 tablespoons butter, melted (optional)

1. In a large mixing bowl combine the warm water and yeast; stir to dissolve yeast. Add 1½ cups of the flour, the sugar, ⅓ cup melted butter, egg, and salt. Beat with an electric mixer on low for 1 minute, scraping sides of bowl constantly. Using a wooden spoon, stir in enough of the remaining flour to make a soft dough that just starts to pull away from sides of bowl (dough will be slightly sticky).
2. Coat a 3-quart covered container with cooking spray. Place dough in container; turn once to grease surface of dough. Cover and chill overnight.
3. Punch dough down. Turn dough out onto a lightly floured surface. Divide dough in half. Cover and let rest for 10 minutes. Meanwhile, lightly grease a 13×9×2-inch baking pan or baking sheets.
4. Shape dough into 24 balls or desired rolls (be careful not to overwork dough; it becomes stickier the more you work with it) and place in the prepared baking pan or 2 to 3 inches apart on the prepared baking sheets. Cover and let rise in a warm place until nearly double in size (about 45 minutes).
5. Preheat oven to 375°F. Bake for 12 to 15 minutes for individual rolls, about 20 minutes for pan rolls, or until golden. Immediately remove rolls from pans. If desired, brush tops of rolls with 2 tablespoons melted butter. Serve warm.

Parmesan-Herb Rosettes Prepare as directed through Step 3, except add ½ teaspoon dried rosemary, crushed, or 1 teaspoon dried thyme or oregano, crushed, to the dough during Step 1. Divide each dough half into 16 pieces. On a lightly floured surface roll each piece into a 12-inch rope. Tie each rope in a loose knot, leaving two long ends. Tuck top end under the knot and bottom end into the top center. Brush with melted butter and sprinkle with grated Parmesan cheese. Place 2 to 3 inches apart on the prepared baking sheets. Continue as directed. Makes 32 rolls.

Salt-and-Pepper Parker House Rolls Prepare as directed through Step 3. On a lightly floured surface roll each dough half until ¼ inch thick. Cut dough with a floured 2½-inch round cutter. Using the dull edge of a table knife, make an off-center crease in each round. Fold each round along the crease; press the folded edge firmly. Place rolls, larger halves up, 2 to 3 inches apart on the prepared baking sheets. Brush with melted butter and sprinkle generously with kosher salt and freshly ground black pepper. Continue as directed. Makes 24 rolls.

PER SERVING 114 cal., 3 g fat (2 g sat. fat), 15 mg chol., 123 mg sodium, 19 g carb., 1 g fiber, 3 g pro.

Double-Cheddar Holiday Biscuits

PREP 20 minutes
BAKE 16 minutes at 425°F
COOL 5 minutes MAKES 5 servings

5 cups unbleached all-purpose flour, sifted before measuring
1 tablespoon plus 1 teaspoon baking powder
2½ teaspoons kosher salt
1 teaspoon granulated sugar
⅛ teaspoon cayenne pepper
1 cup shredded extra-sharp white cheddar cheese, room temperature (4 ounces)
1 cup shredded sharp orange cheddar cheese, room temperature (4 ounces)
6 tablespoons cold unsalted butter, cut into ½-inch pieces
2 cups heavy cream
¼ cup buttermilk

1. Position a rack in the center of the oven. Preheat oven to 425°F. Line a baking sheet with foil. In a large mixing bowl whisk together the flour, baking powder, salt, sugar, and cayenne. Add shredded cheeses, then work in well with your fingers. Add the cold butter. Quickly rub butter into flour mixture with fingers until mixture resembles the texture of oatmeal with some large marble-size pieces.
2. Stir in the heavy cream; add buttermilk and stir just until absorbed. Dough will be chunky and dry at this point. Turn dough out onto a lightly floured board. Using your hand, press and kneed into a cohesive dough.
3. Roll dough to ½-inch thickness. With a fork dipped in flour, prick evenly spaced holes all over the dough. Cut out 2½-inch rounds and place about ½ inch apart on lined baking sheet. Gather dough pieces, reroll, cut out, and place on baking sheet.
4. Bake biscuits for 16 to 18 minutes until well browned, rotating pan if needed to ensure even browning. Cool slightly before serving. (To reheat biscuits, warm them at 350°F for 3 to 5 minutes.)

PER SERVING 197 cal., 12 g fat (7 g sat. fat), 39 mg chol., 259 mg sodium, 18 g carb., 1 g fiber, 5 g pro.

DOUBLE-CHEDDAR HOLIDAY BISCUITS

FENNEL AND
LEEK SOUP

1. For caramelized onions, in a large skillet heat oil over medium heat. Add sliced onion, sugar, and pepper; reduce heat to low and cook, covered, for 30 minutes, stirring twice. Add ginger. Cook, uncovered, 20 to 30 minutes more or until onion is golden brown, stirring occasionally. Divide in half.

2. Meanwhile, peel carrots and sweet potato; cut into 1-inch pieces. In a Dutch oven combine broth, carrots, and sweet potato. Bring to boiling; reduce heat. Simmer, covered, 40 minutes or until vegetables are very tender. Add half of the caramelized onions. Cool slightly. Add vegetable mixture, 2 cups at a time, to a blender or food processor. Cover and blend or process until smooth. Return mixture to saucepan. Add cream; heat through. Season to taste with salt and pepper. Top with remaining caramelized onions.

PER SERVING *105 cal., 5 g fat (2 g sat. fat), 9 mg chol., 524 mg sodium, 13 g carb., 2 g fiber, 2 g pro.*

Harvest Succotash

START TO FINISH 25 minutes
MAKES 8 servings

- 2 slices bacon, chopped
- 1 clove garlic, sliced
- 4 cups finely chopped mustard greens
- 1 12-ounce package frozen corn kernels, thawed (2½ cups)
- 1 10-ounce package frozen lima beans, thawed (2 cups)
- ¾ cup half-and-half or light cream
- 2 tablespoons snipped fresh sage
- ½ teaspoon salt
- ¼ teaspoon black pepper

1. In a very large skillet cook bacon over medium heat until crisp. With a slotted spoon, remove bacon from skillet and drain on paper towels; set aside. Add garlic to skillet. Cook for 30 seconds. Stir in the mustard greens, corn, and beans; cook and stir 3 minutes or until mustard greens soften. Stir in half-and-half, sage, salt, and pepper. Bring to boiling. Transfer to a serving dish. Sprinkle with reserved bacon.

PER SERVING *170 cal., 7 g fat (3 g sat. fat), 15 mg chol., 262 mg sodium, 21 g carb., 4 g fiber, 7 g pro.*

Fennel and Leek Soup

PREP 25 minutes COOK 42 minutes
MAKES 6 servings

- 1 tablespoon butter
- 1 tablespoon olive oil
- 3 fennel bulbs, trimmed, cored, and thinly sliced
- 2 leeks, sliced
- 2 tablespoons dry sherry, vermouth, or white wine
- 3 14.5-ounce cans vegetable broth or chicken broth
- 1 pound russet potatoes, peeled and cut into 1-inch pieces
- 1 teaspoon snipped fresh thyme or ½ teaspoon dried thyme, crushed
  Salt
  Cracked black pepper
  Sautéed sliced leeks (optional)

1. In a 4-quart Dutch oven heat butter and oil over medium heat. Add fennel and 2 leeks; cook about 10 minutes or until crisp-tender, stirring occasionally.

2. Carefully add sherry. Cook and stir about 2 minutes or until sherry is nearly evaporated. Carefully add broth and potatoes. Bring to boiling; reduce heat. Simmer, covered, about 30 minutes or until vegetables are very tender; cool slightly.

3. Transfer fennel mixture in batches to a blender or food processor. Cover and blend or process until smooth. Return pureed mixture to Dutch oven. Stir in thyme; heat through. Season to taste with salt.

4. Ladle soup into bowls. Sprinkle with pepper and, if desired, garnish with additional sautéed leeks.

PER SERVING *176 cal., 7 g fat (3 g sat. fat), 8 mg chol., 979 mg sodium, 28 g carb., 7 g fiber, 4 g pro.*

Ginger-Carrot Soup

PREP 30 minutes COOK 50 minutes
MAKES 12 servings

- 2 tablespoons vegetable oil
- 3 cups thinly sliced onion
- 2 tablespoons sugar
- ⅛ teaspoon black pepper
- 2 tablespoons grated fresh ginger
- 8 carrots (about 1¼ pounds)
- 1 sweet potato
- 6 cups chicken broth
- 1 cup half-and-half or light cream

HARVEST
SUCCOTASH

BAKED FENNEL
WITH PARMESAN

Baked Fennel with Parmesan

PREP 20 minutes
BAKE 15 minutes at 425°F
COOK 5 minutes
MAKES 8 servings

Butter
3 bulbs fennel, cored and cut into thin wedges
1 small sweet onion, such as Vidalia or Maui, cut into thin wedges
4 cloves garlic, thinly sliced
¼ teaspoon salt
¼ teaspoon black pepper
⅛ teaspoon freshly grated nutmeg
½ cup half-and-half or light cream
½ cup finely shredded Parmesan cheese (2 ounces)
2 tablespoons butter, cut up
¼ cup chopped walnuts, toasted*
1 tablespoon snipped fresh parsley (optional)

1. Preheat oven to 425°F. Butter a 2-quart gratin dish or shallow baking dish; set aside. In a Dutch oven cook fennel and sweet onion in a large amount of boiling salted water about 5 minutes or until softened. Drain well.
2. Spoon drained fennel mixture into the prepared gratin or baking dish. Sprinkle with garlic, salt, pepper, and nutmeg. Drizzle with half-and-half. Sprinkle with Parmesan cheese. Dot with the 2 tablespoons butter.
3. Bake about 15 minutes or until butter is melted and bubbly. Sprinkle with walnuts. If desired, garnish with parsley.
***Tip** To toast nuts, seeds, or shredded coconut, spread pieces in a single layer in a shallow baking pan. Bake in a 350°F oven for 5 to 10 minutes or until pieces are golden brown, stirring once or twice.
PER SERVING *137 cal., 9 g fat (4 g sat. fat), 18 mg chol., 273 mg sodium, 10 g carb., 3 g fiber, 5 g pro.*

Creamed Kale

START TO FINISH 30 minutes
MAKES 7 servings

1¾ pounds fresh kale (about 2 bunches)
¼ cup butter
½ cup chopped onion (1 medium)
4 tablespoons all-purpose flour
1½ cups milk
⅓ cup finely shredded Gruyère cheese or Parmesan cheese
¼ teaspoon salt
⅛ teaspoon ground nutmeg
⅛ teaspoon crushed red pepper (optional)

1. Trim and discard stems from kale. Thoroughly wash and drain. Cut kale into ½-inch-wide ribbons; set aside.
2. For sauce, in a medium skillet melt butter over medium heat. Add onion and cook about 5 minutes or until tender. Stir in flour. Add milk all at once; cook and stir until thickened and bubbly. Cook and stir for 1 minute more. Stir in cheese, salt, nutmeg, and, if desired, crushed red pepper. Keep warm.
3. Meanwhile, bring an 8-quart Dutch oven of lightly salted water to boiling. Gradually add kale to boiling water; cook for 5 minutes or until tender. Drain well; return to Dutch oven. Stir sauce into cooked kale; heat through. Top with additional Parmesan and, if desired, crushed red pepper.
PER SERVING *207 cal., 12 g fat (7 g sat. fat), 33 mg chol., 251 mg sodium, 18 g carb., 3 g fiber, 9 g pro.*

Sautéed Spinach with Raisins and Pine Nuts

START TO FINISH 25 minutes
MAKES 8 servings

¼ cup olive oil
1 cup pine nuts
1 cup raisins or golden raisins
8 cloves garlic, sliced
2 pounds fresh baby spinach
1 teaspoon finely shredded lemon peel
3 tablespoons lemon juice
½ teaspoon salt
½ teaspoon black pepper

1. In an extra-large nonstick skillet heat 1 tablespoon of the oil over medium heat. Add pine nuts; cook and stir for 3 to 5 minutes or until golden. Transfer to a serving bowl.
2. Add another 1 tablespoon of the oil to skillet; heat over medium heat. Add one-third of the raisins and one-third of the garlic. Add one-third of the spinach. Cook for 1 to 2 minutes or until spinach begins to wilt, tossing constantly. Transfer to serving bowl. Repeat two more times with the remaining oil, raisins, garlic, and spinach.
3. Add lemon peel, lemon juice, salt, and pepper to spinach; toss to coat.
PER SERVING *262 cal., 19 g fat (2 g sat. fat), 0 mg chol., 235 mg sodium, 22 g carb., 4 g fiber, 6 g pro.*

SAUTÉED SPINACH WITH RAISINS AND PINE NUTS

**BRAISED BRUSSELS
SPROUTS WITH CRISPY
SHALLOTS**

paper towel-lined plate. Season to taste with additional salt.

4. Gently stir vinegar into sprout mixture. Increase heat to medium-high. Cook, uncovered, about 2 minutes or until most of the liquid is evaporated. Remove from heat. Season to taste with additional salt and pepper. Serve topped with shallots.

*Tip To trim Brussels sprouts, cut off the stems just at the spot where the leaves start to grow. Remove dark green outer leaves until the tender, light green leaves are uniformly exposed.

PER SERVING *182 cal., 11 g fat (4 g sat. fat), 15 mg chol., 580 mg sodium, 17 g carb., 6 g fiber, 6 g pro.*

Roasted Green Beans with Beets, Feta, and Walnuts

PREP **30 minutes**
ROAST **45 minutes at 425°F**
MAKES **8 servings**

    2   pounds fresh green beans, trimmed
    1   pound fresh beets, trimmed, peeled, and cut into thin wedges
    ½   cup sliced shallots (4 medium)
    ¼   cup olive oil
    ½   teaspoon salt
    ½   teaspoon freshly ground black pepper
    ½   cup broken walnuts
    ½   cup crumbled feta cheese (2 ounces)

1. Preheat oven to 425°F. In a large roasting pan combine green beans, beets, and shallots. Drizzle with oil and sprinkle with salt and pepper; toss to coat.

2. Roast, uncovered, for 45 to 50 minutes or until beans and beets are tender, stirring once or twice and adding walnuts during the last 10 to 15 minutes of roasting.

3. To serve, transfer roasted vegetables to a serving platter. Sprinkle with cheese.

PER SERVING *199 cal., 14 g fat (3 g sat. fat), 8 mg chol., 303 mg sodium, 16 g carb., 5 g fiber, 6 g pro.*

Braised Brussels Sprouts with Crispy Shallots

START TO FINISH **40 minutes**
MAKES **6 servings**

    2   pounds Brussels sprouts
    3   tablespoons butter
    1   teaspoon kosher salt
    ½   teaspoon dry mustard
    ¼   cup dry white wine
    ½   cup vegetable broth or mushroom broth
    2   tablespoons olive oil
    1   cup thinly sliced shallots
        Kosher salt
    ¼   cup cider vinegar
        Black pepper

1. Trim Brussels sprouts.* In an extra-large skillet heat butter over medium-high heat. Add Brussels sprouts; toss to coat. Sprinkle with 1 teaspoon salt and dry mustard. Cook and stir for 3 to 5 minutes or until sprouts are light brown.

2. Carefully add wine to skillet, stirring to scrape up any crusty brown bits. Add broth. Reduce heat to medium-low. Cook, covered, for 8 to 10 minutes or just until sprouts are tender, stirring occasionally.

3. Meanwhile, in a large skillet heat oil over medium heat. Add shallots, breaking apart into individual rings. Cook for 10 to 12 minutes or until deep brown and crisp, stirring frequently. Using tongs, transfer shallots to a

ROASTED GREEN
BEANS WITH BEETS,
FETA, AND WALNUTS

FENNEL, APPLE, AND WALNUT SALAD WITH CITRUS VINAIGRETTE

Fennel, Apple, and Walnut Salad with Citrus Vinaigrette

START TO FINISH 25 minutes
MAKES 10 servings

1 recipe Basic Vinaigrette, using cider vinegar in place of white wine vinegar
2 tablespoons orange juice
2 tablespoons honey
1 clove garlic, minced
4 cups curly endive, torn
3 cups thinly sliced fennel (2 medium)
1 cup cubed or thinly sliced tart apple or pear (1 medium)
½ cup coarsely chopped walnuts, toasted (see tip, page 25)
½ cup thinly sliced red onion (1 medium)
½ cup crumbled blue cheese, feta cheese, or goat cheese (chèvre) (2 ounces)
Sea salt flakes
Freshly ground black pepper

1. For dressing, in a screw-top jar combine Basic Vinaigrette, orange juice, honey, and garlic. Cover and shake well.

2. In an extra-large bowl combine endive, fennel, apple, walnuts, red onion, and cheese. Drizzle with dressing; toss gently to coat. Season to taste with salt and pepper. Transfer to a serving platter.

Basic Vinaigrette In a small screw-top jar combine ¼ cup olive oil, 2 tablespoons lemon juice, and 2 tablespoons white wine vinegar. Cover and shake well.

PER SERVING *153 cal., 11 g fat (2 g sat. fat), 5 mg chol., 171 mg sodium, 12 g carb., 3 g fiber, 3 g pro.*

Pear and Arugula Salad

PREP **20 minutes** STAND **15 minutes**
MAKES **8 servings**

- 1 recipe Lemon Vinaigrette
- 2 red Bartlett pears
- 12 cups arugula (about 8 ounces)
- ⅓ cup dry-roasted, salted sunflower kernels
- 2 ounces Parmesan cheese, shaved Shredded lemon peel (optional)

1. Prepare Lemon Vinaigrette. Transfer ¼ cup of the vinaigrette dressing to large bowl. Quarter, core, and seed pears. Cut each quarter into thin slices; add to dressing in bowl. Let stand for 15 minutes.
2. Add arugula to pears; toss lightly to coat. Transfer to serving platter. Top with sunflower kernels, Parmesan, and, if desired, lemon peel. Serve with dressing. Cover and refrigerate remaining vinaigrette up to 1 week.
Lemon Vinaigrette In a bowl combine 1 tablespoon lemon peel, ⅓ cup lemon juice, 1 teaspoon sugar, and ½ teaspoon kosher salt. Gradually whisk in ¾ cup extra virgin olive oil.
PER SERVING *274 cal., 25 g fat (4 g sat. fat), 5 mg chol., 265 mg sodium, 11 g carb., 2 g fiber, 5 g pro.*

Winter Greens Salad with Lemon-Anchovy Vinaigrette

START TO FINISH **20 minutes**
MAKES **6 servings**

- 1 recipe Basic Vinaigrette
- ¼ teaspoon Worcestershire sauce
- 3 anchovy fillets or 1 teaspoon anchovy paste
- ½ teaspoon salt
- 2 cloves garlic
- 8 cups mixed salad greens Freshly ground black pepper

1. For dressing, in a screw-top jar combine Basic Vinaigrette and Worcestershire sauce. Using a mortar and pestle, mash together anchovies, salt, and garlic. Add anchovy mixture to mixture in jar. Cover and shake well.
2. Place salad greens in an extra-large bowl. Drizzle with dressing; toss gently to coat. Sprinkle with pepper.

Basic Vinaigrette In a small screw-top jar combine ¼ cup olive oil, 2 tablespoons lemon juice, and 2 tablespoons white wine vinegar. Cover and shake well.
PER SERVING *95 cal., 9 g fat (1 g sat. fat), 3 mg chol., 258 mg sodium, 3 g carb., 1 g fiber, 1 g pro.*

Roasted Asparagus-Orange Salad

PREP **10 minutes**
ROAST **15 minutes at 400°F**
MAKES **8 servings**

- 2 pounds asparagus spears, trimmed
- 1 tablespoon olive oil
- ¼ teaspoon salt
- 2 oranges
- 1 clove garlic, minced
- 1 teaspoon Dijon mustard
- ½ teaspoon fennel seeds, crushed
- 2 tablespoons olive oil
- 1 tablespoon cider vinegar

1. Preheat oven to 400°F. Place asparagus in a 15×10×1-inch baking pan. Drizzle with oil, sprinkle with salt, and toss to coat. Roast, uncovered, for 15 to 20 minutes, until asparagus is crisp-tender, tossing once. Transfer to a serving platter.
2. Meanwhile, for dressing, shred enough peel from 1 orange to equal 1 teaspoon. Juice half an orange. Peel, then slice the remaining half and whole orange half in rounds. In a jar with a tight-fitting lid combine orange peel, orange juice, garlic, mustard, fennel seeds, olive oil, and vinegar. Cover with lid and shake to combine.
3. Drizzle a little of the dressing on the asparagus; toss to coat. Toss in orange slices. Pass any remaining dressing.
PER SERVING *85 cal., 5 g fat (1 g sat. fat), 0 mg chol., 90 mg sodium, 8 g carb., 3 g fiber, 3 g pro.*

WINTER GREENS SALAD
WITH LEMON-ANCHOVY
VINAIGRETTE

CRAB RANGOON
STRUDEL, PAGE 35

Small Bites

FORK-FREE FARE Casual and carefree, finger food encourages social interaction. Guests can load up their plates with tasty tidbits—dips, spreads, meatballs, wings, and crostini—then mingle and chat as they nibble and nosh.

BANGKOK CHILI WINGS

Spicy Apple-Glazed Meatballs

PREP 20 minutes COOK 12 minutes
STAND 10 minutes
MAKES 12 servings

- 1   egg
- ¼   cup milk
- 2   slices white or whole wheat bread, torn
- 1   pound 85% lean ground beef
- 4   cloves garlic, minced
- ½   teaspoon freshly ground black pepper
- ¼   teaspoon salt
- ¼   teaspoon cayenne pepper
- 1   tablespoon vegetable oil
- 1   cup apple juice or pear nectar
- ¼   reduced-sodium soy sauce
- 3   tablespoons packed brown sugar
- 1½ teaspoons cornstarch
- 1   teaspoon ground ginger
- ¼   teaspoon cayenne pepper
- 6   green onions, chopped

1. For spicy meatballs, in a large bowl whisk together egg and milk. Add bread. Let stand 10 minutes, just until bread is softened. Add beef, garlic, black pepper, salt, and cayenne pepper. Mix thoroughly with hands or wooden spoon. Shape beef mixture into forty-eight 1-inch meatballs.
2. In a very large skillet heat oil over medium heat. Cook meatballs, half at a time, about 6 minutes per batch, turning occasionally until brown and crusty on outside and no longer pink inside. Transfer meatballs to a covered dish; cover to keep warm. Drain fat from skillet; wipe out skillet.
3. For apple glaze, in a small bowl combine apple juice, soy sauce, brown sugar, cornstarch, ginger, and cayenne pepper. In same skillet as meatballs were cooked cook and stir juice mixture until thickened and bubbly (at full boil). Cook and stir 2 minutes more. Return meatballs to skillet to heat through and coat with sauce. Transfer glazed meatballs to a serving dish. Top with green onions.
PER SERVING 143 cal., 8 g fat (3 g sat. fat), 42 mg chol., 297 mg sodium, 10 g carb., 0 g fiber, 9 g pro.

Bangkok Chili Wings

PREP 25 minutes COOK 15 minutes
MAKES 12 servings

- 12 chicken wings (about 2½ pounds total)
- 1   tablespoon kosher salt
- 2   tablespoons vegetable oil
- 1   medium mango, seeded, peeled, and cut up
- ½   of a 14-ounce can unsweetened light coconut milk
- 1   tablespoon Asian chili sauce (Sriracha sauce)
- 1   tablespoon lime juice
     Salt
     Mango slices (optional)
     Snipped fresh cilantro (optional)

1. Cut off and discard tips of chicken wings. Cut wings at joints to form 24 pieces. Sprinkle with kosher salt.

In an extra-large skillet heat oil over medium-high heat. Add chicken wings; cook about 10 minutes or until brown on both sides. Drain off fat.
2. For sauce, place cut-up mango in a food processor or blender. Cover and process or blend until smooth. Transfer to a small bowl. Stir in coconut milk, Asian chili sauce, and lime juice. Pour sauce over chicken wings.
3. Bring to simmering. Cook, covered, for 5 minutes. Cook, uncovered, about 10 minutes more or until chicken is no longer pink and sauce is slightly thickened, stirring occasionally and reducing heat as necessary. Season to taste with salt.
4. Transfer to a serving platter. If desired, garnish with mango slices and cilantro.
PER SERVING 151 cal., 11 g fat (3 g sat. fat), 39 mg chol., 586 mg sodium, 4 g carb., 0 g fiber, 9 g pro.

SPICY APPLE-GLAZED
MEATBALLS

An appetizer buffet offers something for everyone. Serve a balanced menu of textures, temperatures, and recipe types.

QUICK-ROASTED SALT AND PEPPER SHRIMP

Lamb Meatballs with Pomegranate Sauce

PREP 35 minutes
BAKE 15 minutes at 300°F
MAKES 6 servings

  1 egg, lightly beaten
  1 cup fine dry bread crumbs
  ¼ cup chopped fresh mint
  2 to 3 cloves garlic, minced
  ½ teaspoon salt
  ¼ teaspoon black pepper
  2 pounds ground lamb
  1 16-ounce bottle pomegranate juice
  1 teaspoon sugar
  3 tablespoons olive oil
1½ cups plain Greek yogurt
  2 tablespoons snipped fresh chives
  1 garlic, minced
     Fresh mint leaves (optional)
     Toasted pita bread wedges (optional)

1. Preheat oven to 300°F. In large bowl combine egg, bread crumbs, mint, 2 or 3 cloves garlic, salt, and pepper. Add ground lamb; mix well. Shape into 32 meatballs; set aside.
2. For sauce, in medium saucepan bring pomegranate juice to boiling; reduce heat. Simmer, uncovered, 25 minutes or until reduced to about ½ cup. Add sugar; stir to dissolve.
3. Meanwhile, in large skillet brown half the meatballs at a time in hot olive oil, turning to brown evenly. Transfer to a 15×10×1-inch baking pan. Bake 15 to 20 minutes or until an instant-read thermometer registers 160°F. In medium bowl combine yogurt, 1 tablespoon of the chives, and 1 clove garlic. To serve, drizzle meatballs with pomegranate sauce; sprinkle with remaining chives and mint (if using). Serve with seasoned yogurt and, if desired, pita wedges.
PER SERVING *695 cal., 50 g fat (21 g sat. fat), 156 mg chol., 449 mg sodium, 27 g carb., 1 g fiber, 32 g pro.*

Quick-Roasted Salt and Pepper Shrimp

PREP 20 minutes
ROAST 8 minutes at 400°F
MAKES 8 servings

CRAB RANGOON STRUDEL

  2 pounds fresh or frozen jumbo shrimp in shells
  1 tablespoon olive oil
  ¾ teaspoon freshly ground black pepper
  ½ teaspoon kosher salt

1. Preheat oven to 400°F. Thaw shrimp, if frozen. Peel and devein shrimp, leaving tails intact if desired. Rinse shrimp; pat dry with paper towels.
2. Place shrimp in a 15×10×1-inch baking pan. Drizzle with oil; sprinkle with pepper and salt. Toss to coat. Roast, uncovered, for 8 to 10 minutes or until shrimp are opaque.
PER SERVING *96 cal., 3 g fat (0 g sat. fat), 143 mg chol., 765 mg sodium, 1 g carb., 15 g pro.*

Crab Rangoon Strudel

PREP 20 minutes
BAKE 22 minutes at 400°F
STAND 5 minutes
MAKES 10 servings

  1 3-ounce package cream cheese, softened
  1 tablespoon milk
  1 6-ounce can crabmeat, drained, flaked, and cartilage removed
  4 green onions, thinly sliced
  1 teaspoon finely shredded lemon peel
  1 frozen puff pastry sheet (½ of a 17.3-ounce package), thawed
  1 recipe Cilantro Dipping Sauce or ⅔ cup purchased sweet-and-sour sauce

1. Preheat oven to 400°F. Line a large baking sheet with parchment paper. For filling, in a large bowl stir together cream cheese and milk. Add crab, green onions, and lemon peel; stir until well combined. Set aside.
2. On a lightly floured surface, unfold puff pastry sheet. Roll pastry sheet into a 10-inch square. Spread crab filling evenly over puff pastry sheet, leaving 1 inch unfilled around outside edges of square. Roll up square; pinch dough to seal seams. If necessary, place roll in freezer about 30 minutes or until firm enough to slice.
3. Using a serrated knife, cut roll into 10 equal pieces. Arrange, cut sides down, on the prepared baking sheet.
4. Bake for 22 to 25 minutes or until golden brown. Let stand for 5 minutes before serving. Serve with Cilantro Dipping Sauce.
Cilantro Dipping Sauce In a large screw-top jar combine ½ cup snipped fresh cilantro, ⅓ cup rice vinegar, 2 tablespoons sesame oil or canola oil, 2 tablespoons honey, 1 tablespoon thinly sliced green onion, and 1 tablespoon horseradish mustard. Cover and shake well.
PER SERVING *118 cal., 8 g fat (3 g sat. fat), 26 mg chol., 104 mg sodium, 7 g carb., 0 g fiber, 5 g pro.*

Drunken Cremini Mushrooms with Sage Crostini

PREP 20 minutes
BAKE 8 minutes at 425°F
MAKES 20 servings

    1 8-ounce loaf baguette-style
       French bread
       Olive oil (optional)
    3 cloves garlic, minced
    3 tablespoons butter or olive oil
   12 ounces fresh cremini or button
       mushrooms, chopped or sliced
   ⅓   cup dry white wine
       Salt
       Black pepper
       Snipped fresh sage or chives
       (optional)

1. Preheat oven to 425°F. Using a serrated knife, diagonally slice the bread. Arrange bread slices on two large baking sheets. If desired, brush each slice lightly with olive oil. Bake for 8 to 10 minutes or until light brown, turning slices over once halfway through baking.

2. In a large skillet cook garlic in hot butter over medium heat for 1 minute. Add mushrooms; cook for 6 to 8 minutes or until mushrooms are tender and most of the liquid has evaporated, stirring occasionally. Remove skillet from heat; add wine. Return skillet to heat. Simmer, uncovered, for 4 to 5 minutes or until liquid is nearly evaporated. Season with salt and pepper to taste. Spoon mushroom mixture onto toasts. If desired, sprinkle with sage.

PER SERVING *50 cal., 2 g fat (1 g sat. fat), 5 mg chol., 105 mg sodium, 6 g carb., 0 g fiber, 1 g pro.*

Roma Tomato Jam and Manchego Cheese Bruschetta

PREP 45 minutes ROAST 1 hour
COOK 1 hour COOL 2 hours
BROIL 3 minutes MAKES 24 servings

    5 pounds roma tomatoes, halved
       lengthwise
    2 tablespoons olive oil
    3 inches stick cinnamon
    3 whole cardamom pods
    5 whole cloves
   ½   cup dry red wine, such as Rioja
    3 tablespoons honey
    2 tablespoons balsamic vinegar
       Kosher salt
   24 ½-inch slices baguette-style
       French bread
    8 ounces Manchego cheese, thinly
       sliced
       Basil leaves (optional)

1. Preheat oven to 350°F. Line two 15×10×1-inch baking pans with parchment paper. Place tomatoes, cut sides down, in the baking pans. Brush with oil. Roast about 1 hour or until skins begin to wrinkle and brown.

2. Remove skins from tomatoes; scrape out seeds. Place tomatoes, half at a time, in a food processor. Cover and process until slightly chunky.

3. For the spice bag, place stick cinnamon, cardamom, and cloves in the center of a double-thick, 6-inch square of 100%-cotton cheesecloth. Bring up corners; tie closed with clean kitchen string.

4. In a large heavy saucepan combine tomatoes, spice bag, wine, honey, and vinegar. Bring to boiling; reduce heat. Simmer, uncovered, about 1 hour or until mixture reaches a thick jamlike consistency, stirring frequently. Remove from heat; remove and discard spice bag. Season to taste with kosher salt. Cool for 2 hours.

5. Preheat broiler. Place baguette slices on a baking sheet. Broil 3 to 4 inches from the heat about 1 minute or until light brown. Top with cheese. Broil about 2 minutes or until cheese is softened. Top with about 1 tablespoon tomato jam and, if desired, basil leaves.

PER SERVING *121 cal., 4 g fat (2 g sat. fat), 8 mg chol., 281 mg sodium, 15 g carb., 1 g fiber, 5 g pro.*

ROMA TOMATO JAM AND MANCHEGO CHEESE BRUSCHETTA

DRUNKEN CREMINI
MUSHROOMS WITH
SAGE CROSTINI

JALAPEÑO CRAB
AND CORN DIP

Jalapeño Crab and Corn Dip

PREP 30 minutes
BAKE 15 minutes at 425°F
MAKES 28 servings

   2 tablespoons butter
   1 cup frozen whole kernel corn
   ½ cup chopped red sweet pepper
      (1 small)
   1 clove garlic, minced
   ½ cup sour cream
   ½ cup mayonnaise
   ½ cup sliced pickled jalapeños,
      drained and chopped
   1 teaspoon Worcestershire sauce
   1 teaspoon bottled hot pepper
      sauce (optional)
   2 6- to 6.5-ounce cans crabmeat,
      drained, flaked, and cartilage
      removed
   1 cup shredded Monterey Jack
      cheese (4 ounces)
   2 tablespoons grated Parmesan
      cheese
      Tortilla chips

1. Preheat oven to 425°F. In a seasoned
or generously greased 8- to 9-inch
cast-iron skillet heat butter over
medium heat until melted. Add corn,
sweet pepper, and garlic; cook about
5 minutes or until tender.
2. In a medium bowl combine sour
cream, mayonnaise, jalapeños,
Worcestershire sauce, and, if desired
hot pepper sauce. Stir in corn mixture,
crabmeat, and Monterey Jack cheese.
Transfer to the cast-iron skillet.
3. Sprinkle crab mixture with
Parmesan cheese. Bake about
15 minutes or until golden and bubbly
around the edge. Serve dip with
tortilla chips.
PER SERVING *74 cal., 6 g fat (2 g sat.
fat), 20 mg chol., 124 mg sodium, 2 g carb.,
0 g fiber, 3 g pro.*

Roasted Vegetable Dip

PREP 20 minutes
ROAST 40 minutes at 425°F
MAKES 8 servings

   4 medium carrots, cut into 1-inch
      pieces
   2 large red sweet peppers, seeded
      and cut into 1-inch pieces

ROASTED
VEGETABLE DIP

   2 medium shallots, halved
   3 cloves garlic
   1 tablespoon olive oil
   ½ teaspoon black pepper
   ¼ teaspoon salt
   2 tablespoons balsamic vinegar
   1 teaspoon snipped fresh rosemary
      Fresh rosemary sprig (optional)
  48 water crackers and/or 8 cups
      assorted vegetables (such as
      broccoli florets, cauliflower
      florets, and/or zucchini sticks)

1. Preheat oven to 425°F. Line a
shallow roasting pan with foil. Place
carrots, red sweet peppers, shallots,
and garlic in prepared pan. Drizzle
with olive oil and sprinkle with black
pepper and salt. Cover with foil.
2. Roast for 20 minutes. Uncover and
stir vegetables. Roast, uncovered, for
20 to 25 minutes or until vegetables
are tender and lightly browned. Cool
slightly on a wire rack.
3. Transfer vegetable mixture to
a food processor. Add vinegar and
the 1 teaspoon rosemary. Cover and
process until smooth. Garnish with a
rosemary sprig, and, if desired, serve
with crackers or vegetables.
PER SERVING *136 cal., 4 g fat (0 g sat.
fat), 217 mg sodium, 24 g carb., 3 g fiber,
3 g pro.*

Marinated Mozzarella with Basil

PREP 15 minutes MARINATE 1 hour
MAKES 14 servings

   ¼ cup fresh basil leaves
   ¼ cup olive oil
   1 teaspoon coarsely ground black
      pepper
   1 to 2 teaspoons balsamic vinegar
   1 pound fresh mozzarella cheese,
      cut into 1-inch cubes
      Tomato slices (optional)
      Baguette slices or crackers

1. Set aside several whole basil leaves
for garnish. Using a sharp knife,
chop the remaining basil leaves. In a
medium bowl combine chopped basil,
oil, pepper, and vinegar. Add cheese
cubes to herb-oil mixture, tossing
gently until cheese is well-coated.
Cover and chill for at least 1 hour.
2. Transfer cheese to a serving dish;
garnish with the reserved whole basil
leaves and, if desired, tomato slices.
Serve with baguette slices or crackers.
PER SERVING *100 cal., 7 g fat (4 g sat.
fat), 18 mg chol., 120 mg sodium, 1 g carb.,
0 g fiber, 8 g pro.*

SPICY ROAST
ALMONDS

Spicy Roast Almonds

PREP **10 minutes**
BAKE **17 minutes at 350°F**
MAKES **12 servings**

- 3 cups whole almonds
- 1 tablespoon butter
- 1 tablespoon olive oil
- 2 tablespoons Worcestershire sauce
- 1 teaspoon ground cumin
- 1 teaspoon garlic powder
- ½ teaspoon kosher salt
- ½ teaspoon cayenne pepper

1. Preheat oven to 350°F. Spread almonds in an even layer in a 15×10×1-inch baking pan. Bake about 10 minutes or until lightly toasted, stirring once.
2. Meanwhile, in a small saucepan heat butter and oil over medium-low heat. Stir in Worcestershire sauce, cumin, garlic powder, salt, and cayenne pepper. Drizzle over almonds; toss

gently to coat. Bake for 7 minutes more. Spread nuts on a large sheet of foil and let cool.
PER SERVING *229 cal., 20 g fat (2 g sat. fat), 3 mg chol., 116 mg sodium, 7 g carb., 4 g fiber, 8 g pro.*

Apple Cider Punch

START TO FINISH **5 minutes**
MAKES **15 servings**

- 6 cups apple cider
- 2 cups orange juice, cranberry-raspberry juice, or orange-mango juice
- ½ cup lemon juice
- 1 750-milliliter bottle sparkling white grape juice*

1. In punch bowl or large pitcher combine apple cider, orange juice, and lemon juice. Slowly add sparkling white grape juice or sparkling wine. Serve immediately.

*****Tip** For an adult punch, use chilled champagne or sparkling wine in place of the sparkling grape juice.
PER SERVING *99 cal., 0 g fat, 0 mg chol., 20 mg sodium, 25 g carb., 0 g fiber, 0 g pro.*

Aztec Hot Chocolate

PREP **15 minutes**
SLOW COOK **4 hours (low) or 2 hours (high)** MAKES **12 servings**

- 4 cups milk
- 2 cups half-and-half or whole milk
- 1 teaspoon instant espresso coffee powder
- 1 teaspoon ground cinnamon
- ½ teaspoon ground chipotle chile pepper
- 1½ cups semisweet chocolate pieces
- 1 recipe Sweetened Whipped Cream (optional)
  Ground cinnamon (optional)

1. In a large bowl combine milk, half-and-half, coffee powder, the 1 teaspoon cinnamon, and the ground chipotle chile pepper. If desired, cover bowl and chill for up to 24 hours.
2. Transfer mixture to a 3½- or 4-quart slow cooker. Stir in chocolate pieces. Cover and cook on low-heat setting for 4 hours or on high-heat setting for 2 hours, whisking vigorously once halfway through cooking time. Serve immediately or keep warm on warm setting or low-heat setting for up to 2 hours.
3. Before serving, whisk well. To serve, ladle beverage into heatproof mugs or cups. If desired, garnish each serving with Sweetened Whipped Cream and/or sprinkle with additional cinnamon.
Sweetened Whipped Cream In a chilled mixing bowl beat 1 cup whipping cream, 2 tablespoons sugar, and ½ teaspoon vanilla with an electric mixer on medium until soft peaks form (tips curl).
PER SERVING *197 cal., 13 g fat (8 g sat. fat), 21 mg chol., 53 mg sodium, 19 g carb., 1 g fiber, 5 g pro.*

AZTEC HOT
CHOCOLATE

SPANISH EGGS,
PAGE 45

Holiday Brunch

RISE AND SHINE! Start the day in a celebratory way with these extra-special morning meals. Wake up and wow guests with homebaked breads and pastries, pancakes, and hearty egg dishes.

IRISH SHEPHERD'S
BREAKFAST PIE

Irish Shepherd's Breakfast Pie

PREP 25 minutes
BAKE 5 minutes at 350°F
MAKES 6 servings

8 eggs, lightly beaten
½ cup milk
¼ teaspoon garlic powder
¼ teaspoon salt
¼ teaspoon black pepper
1 tablespoon butter
½ cup finely chopped onion (1 medium)
½ cup finely chopped red sweet pepper (1 small)
2 cups chopped cooked corned beef*
2 cups prepared mashed potatoes, warmed
¾ cup shredded sharp cheddar cheese (3 ounces)
2 tablespoons snipped fresh parsley

1. Preheat oven to 350°F. In a medium bowl whisk together eggs, milk, garlic powder, salt, and black pepper; set aside.
2. In a large skillet melt butter over medium heat. Add onion and sweet pepper. Cook and stir about 3 minutes or until tender. Add egg mixture. Cook over medium heat, without stirring, until mixture begins to set on bottom and around edges. With a spatula or large spoon, lift and fold the partially cooked egg mixture so the uncooked portion flows underneath. Continue cooking over medium heat until egg mixture is cooked through but is still glossy and moist. Fold in corned beef. Transfer egg mixture to a 2-quart square baking dish.
3. Spoon small mounds of the mashed potatoes over egg mixture. Sprinkle cheese over top. Bake for 5 to 7 minutes or until cheese is melted. Sprinkle with parsley.
*Look for cooked corned beef in the deli section of the grocery store. If you want, use cooked breakfast sausage or ham instead of corned beef.
PER SERVING 375 cal., 24 g fat (11 g sat. fat), 319 mg chol., 1,011 mg sodium, 16 g carb., 2 g fiber, 22 g pro.

SPANISH EGGS

Spanish Eggs

START TO FINISH 35 minutes
MAKES 4 servings

½ cup chopped onion (1 medium)
1 small fresh Anaheim chile, stemmed, seeded, and chopped*
1 clove garlic, minced
1 tablespoon olive oil
4 large tomatoes, chopped
1 small zucchini, halved lengthwise and thinly sliced
1 teaspoon dried savory or cilantro, crushed
½ teaspoon salt
4 eggs
Crumbled queso fresco
Fresh cilantro sprigs (optional)
Corn tortillas, warmed (optional)

1. In a large skillet cook onion, chile, and garlic in hot oil over medium heat about 5 minutes or until tender. Add tomatoes, zucchini, dried savory, and salt; cook about 5 minutes or until tomatoes release their liquid and zucchini is tender.
2. Break 1 egg into a measuring cup. Carefully slide egg into the tomato mixture. Repeat with remaining 3 eggs. Cover and simmer over medium-low heat for 3 to 5 minutes or until whites are completely set and yolks begin to thicken but are not hard. Sprinkle with queso fresco. If desired, garnish with fresh cilantro sprigs and/or serve with corn tortillas.
PER SERVING 176 cal., 10 g fat (3 g sat. fat), 191 mg chol., 395 mg sodium, 13 g carb., 3 g fiber, 11 g pro.
*Tip Fresh chile peppers contain oils that can burn your skin and eyes. When handling them wear disposable plastic or rubber gloves. If your hands do touch the chiles, wash hands and nails thoroughly with soap and water.

Easy Hash Brown Bake

PREP **30 minutes**
BAKE **45 minutes at 350°F**
MAKES **12 servings**

¼ cup vegetable oil
1 32-ounce package loose-pack frozen diced hash brown potatoes
½ cup chopped onion (1 medium)
1 10.75-ounce can condensed cream of chicken soup
1 16-ounce carton light sour cream
2 cups diced cooked ham
8 ounces American cheese,* cubed
¼ teaspoon black pepper
2 cups crushed cornflakes
¼ cup butter or margarine, melted

1. Preheat oven to 350°F. In a large ovenproof skillet heat oil over medium-high heat. Cook potatoes in hot oil for 7 minutes. Stir in onion; cook about 3 minutes more or until some of the potatoes are lightly browned. Stir in soup. Add sour cream, ham, cheese, and pepper, stirring until well mixed. Spoon into a 3-quart baking dish.
2. In a medium bowl stir together cornflakes and melted butter; sprinkle over potato mixture. Bake, uncovered, for 45 to 50 minutes or until hot and bubbly.
*Buy a chunk of American cheese from a deli.

PER SERVING *366 cal., 22 g fat (10 g sat. fat), 58 mg chol., 1,002 mg sodium, 29 g carb., 2 g fiber, 13 g pro.*

Monte Cristo French Toast with Sautéed Apples and Dijon Cream Sauce

PREP **40 minutes**
BAKE **15 minutes at 400°F**
MAKES **4 servings**

Nonstick cooking spray
2 eggs
½ cup milk
1 tablespoon sugar
1 teaspoon vanilla
12 bias-cut 1-inch-thick slices baguette-style French bread (about 6 ounces total)
1 tablespoon butter
1½ cups shredded Swiss cheese (6 ounces)
4 ounces thinly sliced cooked ham, coarsely chopped
2 tablespoons snipped fresh parsley
½ teaspoon dry mustard
2 tablespoons butter
1 medium tart cooking apple, cored and thinly sliced
1 recipe Dijon Cream Sauce

1. Preheat oven to 400°F. Coat a 3-quart rectangular baking dish with cooking spray; set aside.
2. In a shallow bowl beat together eggs, milk, sugar, and vanilla. Dip baguette slices into egg mixture, turning to coat both sides (let soak in egg mixture about 10 seconds per side).
3. In a very large skillet or on a griddle melt the 1 tablespoon butter over medium heat. Add the baguette slices; cook for 4 to 6 minutes or until golden brown, turning once halfway through cooking time. Arrange toast slices in a single layer in the prepared baking dish.
4. In a medium bowl combine cheese, ham, parsley, and dry mustard. Top toast slices with the cheese-ham mixture, mounding and lightly packing it on top. Bake for 15 to 20 minutes or until tops are golden brown and bubbly.
5. Meanwhile, in a medium saucepan melt the 2 tablespoons butter over medium heat. Add apple slices; cook for 5 to 6 minutes or until apples are tender.
6. Top toast slices with apples slices. Drizzle with Dijon Cream Sauce.
Dijon Cream Sauce In a small saucepan melt 1 tablespoon butter over medium heat. Stir in 1 tablespoon all-purpose flour, ⅛ teaspoon salt, and dash black pepper. Stir in ¾ cup milk. Cook and stir over medium heat until thickened and bubbly. Cook and stir for 1 minute more. Stir in 1 tablespoon Dijon mustard and ½ teaspoon snipped fresh thyme.

PER SERVING *575 cal., 30 g fat (16 g sat. fat), 182 mg chol., 1,108 mg sodium, 45 g carb., 3 g fiber, 29 g pro.*

EASY HASH BROWN BAKE

MONTE CRISTO
FRENCH TOAST WITH
SAUTÉED APPLES AND
DIJON CREAM SAUCE

CORNMEAL AND SAUSAGE BREAKFAST SCONES

Cornmeal and Sausage Breakfast Scones

PREP 25 minutes
BAKE 18 minutes at 375°F
COOL 5 minutes
MAKES 8 servings

    Nonstick cooking spray
1 14-ounce package precooked brown and serve breakfast sausage links, thawed
½ cup sour cream
½ teaspoon baking soda
⅔ cup yellow cornmeal
1⅓ cups all-purpose flour
¼ cup granulated sugar
2 teaspoons baking powder
½ teaspoon garlic salt
1 teaspoon Italian seasoning
6 tablespoons butter, cold
1 egg, lightly beaten
¼ cup coarsely chopped roasted red pepper
3 tablespoons butter, melted
⅓ cup (grated or finely shredded) Parmesan cheese
¾ teaspoon Italian seasoning

1. Preheat oven to 375°F. Spray a 12×17-inch baking sheet with nonstick cooking spray. Set aside. Coarsely chop sausage links; place in a small microwave-safe bowl and heat until warm, about 30 to 45 seconds. Set aside.
2. In a small bowl combine sour cream and baking soda. Set aside.
3. Place cornmeal, flour, sugar, baking powder, garlic salt, and 1 teaspoon Italian seasoning in a food processor. Pulse until just combined. Cut 6 tablespoons cold butter into small pieces and add to flour mixture in processor bowl. Process until mixture resembles coarse crumbs.
4. Place flour mixture in a large bowl and add egg, sour cream mixture, and red pepper. Using a rubber spatula, toss together until evenly distributed. Mixture will be dry. Using your hands, add the warm sausage and toss together, kneading gently, until sausage is completely incorporated. Form the dough into a ball and place on a lightly floured surface. Press evenly to about 1 inch thick.

5. In a small bowl combine 3 tablespoons melted butter, Parmesan cheese, and ¾ teaspoon Italian seasoning. Spread evenly over flattened dough. Cut dough into 8 to 10 scones. Place on prepared baking sheet ½ inch apart. Bake on middle rack in oven for 18 to 20 minutes or until raised, firm and lightly golden brown. Remove pan from oven and let cool 5 minutes before serving.
PER SERVING *495 cal., 34 g fat (16 g sat. fat), 103 mg chol., 969 mg sodium, 34 g carb., 1 g fiber, 14 g pro.*

Banana-Multigrain Streusel Muffins

PREP 25 minutes
BAKE 20 minutes at 375°F
COOL 5 minutes
MAKES 20 servings

    Nonstick cooking spray
¼ cup canola oil
¼ cup reduced-fat creamy peanut butter
½ cup packed brown sugar
1 egg
1 cup whole bran cereal
1 cup mashed very ripe bananas (about 3 medium)
¼ cup light sour cream
1 tablespoon vanilla
1 cup all-purpose flour
½ cup whole wheat flour
2 tablespoons flaxseed meal
2 teaspoons baking powder
1 teaspoon ground nutmeg
½ teaspoon salt
1 cup buttermilk or sour milk*
1 recipe Streusel Crunch Topping

1. Preheat oven to 375°F. Line twenty to twenty-two 2½-inch muffin cups with paper bake cups. Lightly coat bake cups with cooking spray. (Or coat muffin cups with cooking spray.) Set aside. In a large bowl combine oil and peanut butter. Beat with an electric mixer on medium for 30 seconds. Add brown sugar, beating until combined. Add egg, cereal, bananas, sour cream, and vanilla; beat just until combined. Set aside. In a medium bowl combine all-purpose flour, whole wheat flour, flaxseed meal, baking powder, nutmeg, and salt. Alternately add flour mixture and buttermilk to banana mixture,

beating on low after each addition just until combined.
2. Spoon batter into prepared muffin cups, filling each about three-fourths full. Sprinkle Streusel Crunch Topping evenly over batter in muffin cups.
3. Bake about 20 minutes or until lightly browned and muffin tops spring back when lightly touched. Cool in muffin cups on a wire rack for 5 minutes. Remove from muffin cups.
Streusel Crunch Topping In a large bowl combine ¼ cup all-purpose flour, ¼ cup rolled oats, ¼ cup packed brown sugar, and ¼ teaspoon ground cinnamon. Add 3 tablespoons canola oil, stirring until combined.
***Tip** To make 1 cup sour milk, place 1 tablespoon lemon juice or vinegar in a glass measuring cup. Add enough milk to make 1 cup total liquid; stir. Let stand for 5 minutes before using.
PER SERVING *172 cal., 7 g fat (1 g sat. fat), 12 mg chol., 143 mg sodium, 24 g carb., 3 g fiber, 4 g pro.*

BANANA-MULTIGRAIN STREUSEL MUFFINS

Blueberry-Ricotta Pancakes

PREP 20 minutes   COOK 2 minutes
per batch   MAKES 2 servings

- ½ cup all-purpose flour
- 2 teaspoons baking powder
- ½ teaspoon salt
- 1 cup ricotta cheese
- 4 egg yolks
- 3 tablespoons sugar
- ¼ cup milk
- 1½ cups fresh or frozen blueberries
- 4 egg whites
- 1 recipe Blueberry Syrup (optional)

1. In a large bowl combine flour, baking powder, and salt. In a medium bowl whisk together ricotta cheese, egg yolks, and sugar until well mixed. Add ricotta mixture to flour mixture; stir until smooth. Stir in milk. Fold in blueberries.
2. In a small bowl beat egg whites with an electric mixer on high until stiff peaks form (tips stand straight). Gently fold beaten egg whites into batter, leaving a few puffs of egg white. Do not overbeat.
3. For each pancake, pour about ¼ cup of the batter onto a hot, lightly greased griddle or heavy skillet. Spread batter into a circle about 4 inches in diameter. Cook over medium heat for 1 to 2 minutes per side or until pancakes are golden brown, turning to second sides when surfaces are bubbly and edges are slightly dry. Serve immediately or keep warm in a loosely covered baking dish in a 300°F oven. If desired, serve with Blueberry Syrup.
PER SERVING *72 cal., 3 g fat (1 g sat. fat), 58 mg chol., 150 mg sodium, 8 g carb., 0 g fiber, 4 g pro.*

Blueberry Syrup In a medium saucepan combine 2 cups fresh or frozen blueberries, 1 cup pure maple syrup, and 2 teaspoons lime or lemon juice. Bring to boiling; reduce heat. Simmer, uncovered, for 15 to 20 minutes or until blueberries become soft, stirring occasionally. Use a potato masher to thoroughly mash blueberries. Set a fine-mesh sieve over a bowl; pour blueberry pulp through sieve. Discard solids. Serve warm.

Blueberry Cream Cheese Pastries

PREP 30 minutes
BAKE 15 minutes at 400°F
MAKES 12 servings

- 1 8-ounce package cream cheese, softened
- ⅓ cup sugar
- 1 teaspoon lemon juice
- 1 teaspoon vanilla
- 1 cup fresh or frozen blueberries
- ½ cup blueberry preserves
- 1 17.3-ounce package frozen puff pastry sheets (2 sheets), thawed
- 1 egg
- 1 tablespoon water

1. Preheat oven to 400°F. Line two large baking sheets with parchment paper
2. In a medium bowl beat cream cheese with an electric mixer on medium until smooth. Add sugar, lemon juice, and vanilla. Beat until well mixed; set aside. In a small bowl stir together blueberries and blueberry preserves; set aside.
3. On a lightly floured surface roll each sheet of the thawed puff pastry into a 10-inch square. Cut each square into six rectangles (each about 5×3½ inches). Transfer rectangles to prepared baking sheets. Using a fork, prick the center of each rectangle, leaving a ½-inch unpricked border around all the edges. In a small bowl beat egg and the water together with a fork. Brush rectangles with egg mixture. Spread a well-rounded tablespoon of the cream cheese mixture onto the center of each rectangle, leaving a ½-inch border. Top each with 2 rounded teaspoons of the blueberry mixture, spreading evenly over cream cheese mixture.
4. Bake for 15 to 18 minutes or until golden brown. Transfer to wire racks. Cool completely.
PER SERVING *316 cal., 20 g fat (4 g sat. fat), 36 mg chol., 224 mg sodium, 32 g carb., 1 g fiber, 3 g pro.*

BLUEBERRY-RICOTTA
PANCAKES

STREUSEL-TOPPED
BERRY-ORANGE ROLLS

Streusel-Topped Berry-Orange Rolls

PREP 20 minutes STAND 1 hour
COOL 5 minutes BAKE 18 minutes at
350°F MAKES 18 servings

- 9 frozen orange spiral-shape rolls, such as Rhodes brand
- 3 cups fresh or frozen mixed berries, such as raspberries, blueberries, and/or blackberries*
- ⅓ cup orange marmalade
- 6 tablespoons all-purpose flour
- ¼ cup packed brown sugar
- 2 tablespoons granulated sugar
- ½ teaspoon ground cinnamon
- ¼ cup butter, cut up
- ¼ cup chopped hazelnuts (filberts) or almonds
- ¼ cup coconut

1. Allow frozen rolls to stand at room temperature for 1 hour. Meanwhile, grease eighteen 2½-inch muffin cups; set aside. For filling, in a medium bowl stir together berries and marmalade; set aside.
2. Preheat oven to 350°F. Using a serrated knife, cut each roll in half horizontally. Gently press each roll half onto the bottom and up the sides of a prepared muffin cup. Spoon filling into muffin cups.
3. For topping, in a small bowl stir together flour, brown sugar, granulated sugar, and cinnamon. Using a pastry blender, cut in butter until mixture resembles coarse crumbs. Stir in hazelnuts and coconut. Sprinkle topping over filling.
4. Bake for 18 to 20 minutes or until filling is bubbly and topping is golden. Cool rolls in muffin cups on wire racks for 5 minutes. Carefully remove rolls from muffin cups. Drizzle icing from package over warm rolls; cool completely on wire racks.
*If using frozen berries, thaw and drain before combining with marmalade.
PER SERVING *233 cal., 7 g fat (2 g sat. fat), 7 mg chol., 155 mg sodium, 35 g carb., 2 g fiber, 3 g pro.*

DARK CHOCOLATE, RAISIN, AND NUT GRANOLA

Dark Chocolate, Raisin, and Nut Granola

PREP 25 minutes
BAKE 45 minutes at 325°F
MAKES 18 servings

- ½ cup unsweetened applesauce
- ¼ cup packed brown sugar
- 2 tablespoons unsalted butter
- 2 tablespoons honey
- 1 tablespoon vanilla
- 1 teaspoon sea salt
- 3 cups rolled oats
- ¾ cup pistachio nuts
- ¾ cup slivered almonds
- ½ cup pumpkin seeds (pepitas)
- ½ cup raw sunflower kernels
- 2 tablespoons ground cinnamon
- 1½ cups raisins
- 1 cup dark chocolate pieces

1. Preheat oven to 325°F. In a small saucepan combine applesauce, brown sugar, butter, honey, vanilla, and salt. Cook and stir over low heat until butter is melted and brown sugar is dissolved.
2. In an extra-large bowl combine oats, pistachio nuts, almonds, pumpkin seeds, sunflower kernels, and cinnamon. Drizzle applesauce mixture over oats mixture; stir to coat. Transfer to a 15×10×1-inch baking pan or a shallow roasting pan.
3. Bake for 45 minutes, stirring twice. Stir in raisins. Transfer to an extra-large bowl; cool. Stir in chocolate pieces. Store in an airtight container.
PER SERVING *273 cal., 14 g fat (4 g sat. fat), 4 mg chol., 93 mg sodium, 35 g carb., 4 g fiber, 7 g pro.*

Roasted Breakfast Pears

PREP 15 minutes
BAKE 20 minutes at 350°F
CHILL 2 hours MAKES 4 servings

- 4 large ripe, yet firm, Bosc or red Anjou pears
- 1 tablespoon lemon juice
- 1 tablespoon butter, softened
- 2 tablespoons packed brown sugar
- ¼ teaspoon salt
- ¼ cup orange juice
- 1 teaspoon vanilla
- 1 cup plain Greek yogurt
- 2 teaspoons finely shredded orange peel
- 2 tablespoons pure maple syrup, Finely shredded orange peel (optional)
- ¼ cup granola
- 2 tablespoons sliced almonds, toasted (see tip, page 25)

1. Preheat oven to 350°F. Halve pears; core. Using a melon baller, scoop out a 1-inch depression in the center of each pear. Brush cut sides with lemon juice.
2. Spread butter in the bottom of a 2-quart rectangular baking dish. Sprinkle with brown sugar and salt; add orange juice. Arrange pear halves, cut sides up, in a single layer in the baking dish.
3. Bake for 20 to 30 minutes or just until pears are tender, spooning cooking liquid over pears several times during baking time (baking time depends upon ripeness of pears).
4. Remove from oven; stir vanilla into cooking liquid. Let cool completely.

Cover and chill for at least 2 hours or up to 24 hours, turning pears in liquid at least once during chilling time.
5. To serve, in a small bowl stir together yogurt, orange peel, and maple syrup. Spoon the mixture into each pear half. If desired, sprinkle with additional orange peel. Serve with granola and toasted almonds.

PER SERVING 308 cal., 8 g fat (3 g sat. fat), 11 mg chol., 199 mg sodium, 55 g carb., 8 g fiber, 9 g pro.

Peach Breakfast Gratin

PREP 15 minutes
BAKE 25 minutes at 425°F
STAND 20 minutes
MAKES 6 servings

- ½ cup milk
- 2 eggs
- ½ cup all-purpose flour
- 2 tablespoons sugar
- 2 tablespoons butter, melted
- ½ teaspoon vanilla
- ¼ teaspoon salt
- 4 medium ripe, yet firm, peaches
- ½ cup granola with almonds or pecans
- ½ cup plain Greek yogurt
  Sugar
  Maple syrup

1. Preheat oven to 425°F. In a medium bowl whisk together milk and eggs. Add flour, 2 tablespoons sugar, melted butter, vanilla, and salt, whisking until smooth. Set aside.
2. If desired, peel peaches. Pit and slice peaches.
3. Grease a 9- to 10-inch deep-dish pie plate. Pour batter into pie plate. Arrange peach slices on top of batter.
4. Bake for 20 minutes. Sprinkle with granola. Bake for 5 to 10 minutes more or until batter is lightly browned and set and peaches are tender. Let cool for 20 minutes before serving.
5. Meanwhile, in a small bowl stir together yogurt and enough additional sugar to reach desired sweetness. Serve yogurt mixture with peach gratin. Drizzle individual servings with maple syrup.

PER SERVING 240 cal., 8 g fat (4 g sat. fat), 75 mg chol., 179 mg sodium, 36 g carb., 2 g fiber, 8 g pro.

ROASTED BREAKFAST PEARS

PEACH BREAKFAST
GRATIN

Something special to sip—whether it's spiced hot coffee or a refreshing fruit drink—makes an ordinary meal extraordinary.

ORANGE-MANGO
AGUA FRESCA

Orange-Mango Agua Fresca

START TO FINISH 20 minutes
MAKES 6 servings

- 4 cups peeled, seeded, and cubed ripe mangoes (about 4)
- 1½ cups orange juice (freshly squeezed juice is preferable)
- ¼ cup lime juice (freshly squeezed juice is preferable)
- 1¼ cups water
- 2 tablespoons honey (optional)
  Ice cubes or crushed ice
  Clementine wedges, orange slices, mandarin orange segments, and/or miniature limes

1. In a blender combine mangoes, orange juice, and lime juice. Cover and blend until smooth. Strain mixture through a fine-mesh sieve into a pitcher or large glass jar. Discard solids. Stir in the water and, if desired, honey. Serve immediately or chill until ready to serve.
2. Serve in ice-filled glasses. Garnish with orange slices, clementine or mandarin orange segments, and/or miniature limes.

PER SERVING *72 cal., 0 g fat, 0 mg chol., 5 mg sodium, 18 g carb., 2 g fiber, 1 g pro.*

Good Morning Mulled Punch

START TO FINISH 15 minutes
MAKES 8 servings

- 4 cups apple cider or juice
- 1 cup orange juice
- 1 cup unsweetened pineapple juice
- ⅓ cup lemon juice
- ½ teaspoon whole allspice
  Apple rings and/or fresh mint sprigs (optional)

1. In a large nonreactive saucepan combine cider, orange juice, pineapple juice, lemon juice, and allspice. Heat over medium-high heat for 5 minutes, stirring occasionally.
2. Place a fine-mesh sieve over a large bowl. Carefully strain the cider mixture through the sieve. Discard allspice.

GOOD MORNING MULLED PUNCH

3. Carefully pour the warm cider mixture into eight heatproof mugs. If desired, garnish with apple rings and/or mint sprigs. Serve warm.
PER SERVING *95 cal., 0 g fat, 0 mg chol., 5 mg sodium, 24 g carb., 0 g fiber, 0 g pro.*

Cinnamon Coffee

PREP 20 minutes
STAND 10 minutes
MAKES 4 servings

- 3 tablespoons sugar
- 3 inches stick cinnamon
- 4 cups hot strong coffee
- ¼ cup half-and-half
  Whipped cream (optional)
  Ground cinnamon (optional)

1. Place sugar and the stick cinnamon into coffee pot; brew the 4 cups coffee.
2. Once coffee is brewed, let stand for 10 minutes on the warming element.
3. Pour the coffee into four mugs. Stir 1 tablespoon half-and-half into each mug.
4. If desired top each serving with whipped cream and sprinkle with the ground cinnamon.
PER SERVING *76 cal., 3 g fat (2 g sat. fat), 8 mg chol., 21 mg sodium, 12 g carb., 0 g fiber, 1 g pro.*

Home-Baked Breads

SLICE OF HEAVEN The aroma of bread baking in the oven is warm and welcoming—and that's just the start of the good stuff. This recipe collection offers up breads and pastries both sweet and savory—convenient quick breads and satisfying yeast breads.

STREUSEL APPLE
BREAD, PAGE 70

Vanilla-Glazed Apricot-Oat Bread

PREP 30 minutes RISE 2 hours
BAKE 1 hour 10 minutes at 350°F
COOL 15 minutes
MAKES 16 servings

1¼ cups boiling water
1 cup quick-cooking oats
1 cup dried apricots, snipped into
   ½-inch pieces
⅓ cup butter, cut into small pieces
⅓ cup honey
1¼ teaspoons salt
¼ cup warm water (105°F to 115°F)
1 package active dry yeast
2 eggs
3½ cups all-purpose flour
1 recipe Vanilla Glaze
   Snipped dried apricots and/or
   sliced almonds (optional)

1. In a large mixing bowl stir together the boiling water, oats, and the 1 cup apricots. Add butter, honey, and salt; mix well. Cover and set aside until mixture cools to lukewarm.
2. In a small bowl combine the warm water and yeast; let stand until mixture is foamy. Add yeast mixture, eggs, and 1½ cups of the flour to the oat mixture. Beat with an electric mixer on low until just combined. Beat on medium for 3 minutes, scraping

sides of bowl occasionally. Using a wooden spoon, gradually stir in remaining flour until a soft, sticky dough forms. Cover; let rise in a warm place until nearly double in size (about 1½ hours).
3. Punch dough down. Transfer dough to a greased 3-quart round casserole. Cover; let rise until double in size (about 30 minutes).
4. Preheat oven to 350°F. Bake for 30 minutes. Cover with foil; bake about 40 minutes more or until an instant-read thermometer inserted into the center of the loaf registers 210°F.* (The bottom may get dark, but the flavor will be fine.) Remove from oven. Using a skewer, prick loaf top in 15 to 20 places. Brush Vanilla Glaze generously over the top of the hot loaf in several applications, allowing the glaze to soak into the skewer holes. If desired, garnish bread with snipped apricots and sliced almonds. Let cool in dish for 15 minutes. Remove bread from dish; serve warm or cool completely on a wire rack.
Vanilla Glaze In a medium bowl whisk together 2 cups powdered sugar, 3 tablespoons milk, 1 tablespoon light-color corn syrup, and 1 teaspoon vanilla. Whisk in additional milk, 1 teaspoon at a time, to make glaze drizzling consistency. Makes ¾ cup.
*This bread will not sound hollow when tapped, so it is necessary to take an internal temperature reading to ensure that it is done.

PER SERVING 285 cal., 6 g fat (3 g sat. fat), 37 mg chol., 222 mg sodium, 54 g carb., 2 g fiber, 6 g pro.

Hearty Mixed Grain Bread

PREP 30 minutes
RISE 1 hour 15 minutes
STAND 10 minutes
BAKE 30 minutes at 375°F
MAKES 24 servings

1¼ cups boiling water
½ cup uncooked seven-grain hot
   cereal
3 to 3½ cups all-purpose flour
1 package active dry yeast
¾ cup fat-free milk
¼ cup honey

2 tablespoons canola oil
1½ teaspoons salt
1½ cups whole wheat flour or white
   whole wheat flour
½ cup rolled oats
¼ cup flaxseed meal
   Fat-free milk
¼ cup rolled oats and/or flaxseeds

1. In a medium bowl combine the boiling water and cereal. Let stand for 20 minutes. In a large mixing bowl combine 2 cups of the all-purpose flour and the yeast; set aside. In a small saucepan heat and stir ¾ cup milk, the honey, oil, and salt over medium heat just until warm (120°F to 130°F). Add milk mixture to flour mixture along with cereal mixture. Beat with an electric mixer on low to medium for 30 seconds, scraping sides of bowl. Beat on high for 3 minutes. Using a wooden spoon, stir in whole wheat flour, ½ cup oats, the flaxseed meal, and as much of the remaining all-purpose flour as you can.
2. Turn dough out onto a lightly floured surface. Knead in enough of the remaining all-purpose flour to make a moderately stiff dough that is almost smooth and elastic (6 to 8 minutes total). Shape dough into a ball. Place in a lightly greased bowl, turning once to grease surface of dough. Cover; let rise in a warm place until double in size (45 to 60 minutes).
3. Punch dough down. Turn out onto a lightly floured surface. Divide in half. Cover; let rest for 10 minutes. Lightly grease a large baking sheet; set aside.
4. Shape dough halves into 8-inch-long oval loaves that are about 4 inches wide at the center. Place shaped loaves 4 inches apart on prepared baking sheet. Cover and let rise in a warm place until nearly double in size (about 30 minutes).
5. Preheat oven to 375°F. Brush tops of loaves lightly with milk; sprinkle with ¼ cup oats and/or flaxseeds. Bake for 30 to 35 minutes or until bread sounds hollow when lightly tapped, covering loosely with foil, if necessary, the last 10 minutes of baking to prevent overbrowning. Transfer loaves to wire racks and cool completely.

PER SERVING 142 cal., 2 g fat (0 g sat. fat), 0 mg chol., 151 mg sodium, 26 g carb., 2 g fiber, 4 g pro.

HEARTY MIXED
GRAIN BREAD

APRICOT-CHERRY PANETTONE

Apricot-Cherry Panettone

PREP 35 minutes STAND 20 minutes
RISE 2 hours 15 minutes
COOL 10 minutes
BAKE 50 minutes at 350°F
MAKES 16 servings

⅓ cup snipped dried apricots
⅓ cup dried tart cherries or dried
    cranberries, coarsely chopped
2   tablespoons apricot brandy,
    orange liqueur, or orange juice
¾   cup milk
1   package active dry yeast
2¼ to 2¾ cups bread flour
2   cups eggs
¼   cup granulated sugar
¼   cup butter, softened
½   teaspoon salt
½   cup yellow cornmeal
⅓   cup chopped almonds, toasted
    (see tip, page 25)
2   tablespoons flaxseeds
    Nonstick cooking spray
1   tablespoon water
    Powdered sugar (optional)

1. In a small bowl combine apricots, cherries, and brandy; cover and let stand for 15 minutes, stirring occasionally. In a small saucepan heat milk just until warm (105°F to 115°F). Pour into a large mixing bowl. Sprinkle yeast over milk and let stand for 5 minutes or until the yeast dissolves. Add 1½ cups of the flour, 1 of the eggs, the granulated sugar, butter, and salt. Beat with an electric mixer on low to medium for 30 seconds, scraping sides of bowl constantly. Beat on high for 3 minutes more. Using a wooden spoon, stir in cornmeal, almonds, flaxseeds, undrained apricot mixture, and as much of the remaining flour as you can. Dough should be just stiff enough to knead.

2. Turn dough out onto a floured surface. Knead in enough of the remaining flour to make a moderately soft dough that is smooth and elastic (3 to 5 minutes total). Shape into a ball. Place dough in a large greased bowl, turning once to grease surface of dough. Cover; let rise in a warm place until double in size (1¼ to 1½ hours).

3. Coat a 7-cup panettone mold or 8-inch springform pan with cooking spray; set aside. Or place a 6×4½-inch round panettone paper baking mold* on a baking sheet; set aside.

4. Punch dough down; shape into a ball. Transfer dough to the prepared pan or mold and flatten slightly to fit shape of pan or mold. Cover and let rise until nearly double in size (1 to 1¼ hours).

5. Preheat oven to 350°F. In a small bowl combine the remaining egg and the water; beat together with a fork. Brush over top of loaf. Bake about 50 minutes for panettone pan or mold, 45 minutes for springform pan, or until bread sounds hollow when tapped and internal temperature of the bread reaches 195°F to 200°F on an instant-read thermometer. If necessary, cover top of bread loosely with foil the last 15 to 20 minutes of baking to prevent overbrowning. Cool for 10 minutes in pan on a wire rack. Remove from pan. Cool bread completely. If desired, sprinkle top of bread with powdered sugar.

*Paper baking molds are available in specialty or kitchenware stores or from kingarthurflour.com.

PER SERVING *169 cal., 5 g fat (2 g sat. fat), 8 mg chol., 114 mg sodium, 27 g carb., 2 g fiber, 5 g pro.*

Orange-Scented Beignets with Chocolate-Hazelnut Filling

PREP 40 minutes CHILL 4 hours
STAND 30 minutes MAKES 40 servings

- 3 to 3½ cups all-purpose flour
- 1 package active dry yeast
- ½ teaspoon freshly grated nutmeg or ground nutmeg
- ½ teaspoon finely shredded orange peel
- ¾ cup milk
- ¼ cup granulated sugar
- ¼ cup orange juice
- 2 tablespoons shortening
- ½ teaspoon salt
- 1 egg
  Vegetable oil for deep-fat frying
- 1½ cups chocolate-hazelnut spread
  Powdered sugar (optional)

1. In a large mixing bowl stir together 1½ cups of the flour, the yeast, nutmeg, and orange peel. In a small saucepan heat and stir milk, granulated sugar, orange juice, shortening, and salt just until warm (120°F to 130°F) and shortening almost melts.

2. Add milk mixture to flour mixture. Add egg. Beat with an electric mixer on low for 30 seconds, scraping sides of bowl constantly. Beat on high for 3 minutes. Using a wooden spoon, stir in enough of the remaining flour to make a soft dough.

3. Place dough in a greased bowl, turning once to grease surface. Cover and chill for 4 to 24 hours.

4. Turn dough out onto a lightly floured surface. Cover; let rest for 10 minutes. Roll dough into a 14×12-inch rectangle. Cut rectangle crosswise into five strips. Cut each strip crosswise into eight 1½-inch-wide rectangles, making 40 rectangles total. Cover; let stand for 20 minutes (dough will not double).

5. In a deep saucepan heat 3 inches of oil to 375°F. Fry a few dough rectangles at a time in hot oil about 1 minute or until golden, turning once. Remove with a slotted spoon and drain on paper towels. Keep warm in a 200°F oven while frying the remaining beignets.

6. Fill a pastry bag fitted with a small round tip with chocolate-hazelnut spread. Poke a small hole in one end of each beignet; insert tip of pastry bag. Squeeze to fill with 1 to 2 teaspoons of the spread. If desired, sprinkle beignets generously with powdered sugar.

PER SERVING *114 cal., 6 g fat (3 g sat. fat), 5 mg chol., 37 mg sodium, 12 g carb., 1 g fiber, 2 g pro.*

ORANGE-SCENTED
BEIGNETS WITH
CHOCOLATE-HAZELNUT
FILLING

TIRAMISU LADDER LOAF

Tiramisu Ladder Loaf

PREP **30 minutes** STAND **10 minutes**
RISE **30 minutes**
BAKE **25 minutes at 350°F**
COOL **40 minutes**
MAKES **12 servings**

- 1 1-pound loaf frozen sweet bread dough, thawed
- ½ cup mascarpone cheese
- 1 3-ounce package cream cheese, softened
- 1 egg yolk
- ¼ cup powdered sugar
- 1 tablespoon coffee liqueur or 1 teaspoon instant espresso coffee powder dissolved in 1 tablespoon water
- ¼ cup miniature semisweet chocolate pieces
- 1 tablespoon powdered sugar or 1 tablespoon powdered sugar mixed with ½ teaspoon unsweetened cocoa powder

1. Line a 15×10×1-inch baking pan with parchment paper; set aside. On a lightly floured surface roll dough into a 15×10-inch rectangle. Carefully transfer dough to the prepared baking pan. Cover and let stand for 10 minutes.
2. Meanwhile, for filling, in a small mixing bowl beat mascarpone cheese, cream cheese, and egg yolk with an electric mixer on medium until smooth. Beat in ¼ cup powdered sugar and liqueur.
3. Spread filling in a 4-inch strip down the center of dough to within 1 inch of the ends. Sprinkle with chocolate pieces. On the long sides, make 2½-inch cuts from edges toward center at 1-inch intervals. Starting at one end, alternately fold opposite strips of dough, at an angle, across filling. Lightly press ends together in the center to seal. Cover and let rise in a warm place for 30 minutes.
4. Preheat oven to 350°F. Bake for 25 to 30 minutes or until golden. Cool in pan on a wire rack for at least 40 minutes. Before serving, sprinkle warm loaf with powdered sugar. Store any leftover loaf in the refrigerator.
PER SERVING *221 cal., 11 g fat (5 g sat. fat), 43 mg chol., 226 mg sodium, 26 g carb., 1 g fiber, 7 g pro.*

Lemon-Almond Cream Bread

PREP **25 minutes** BAKE **25 minutes** at 375°F COOL **10 minutes**
MAKES **10 servings**

- ½ cup mascarpone cheese
- 2 tablespoons lemon curd
- 1 tablespoon all-purpose flour
- ½ teaspoon almond extract
- ¼ cup golden raisins
- 1 16-ounce loaf frozen sweet roll dough, thawed
- 1 egg
- 1 teaspoon water
- 1 recipe Lemon Glaze
- 2 tablespoons sliced almonds, toasted (see tip, page 25)

1. Preheat oven to 375°F. Line a very large baking sheet with parchment paper; set aside.
2. For filling, in a small bowl stir together mascarpone cheese, lemon curd, flour, and almond extract. Stir in raisins; set aside.
3. On a lightly floured surface roll dough into a 13×9-inch rectangle, letting dough relax as necessary while rolling. Transfer dough to the prepared baking sheet. Spoon filling lengthwise down the center of the dough, spreading into a 2½-inch-wide strip. Using kitchen scissors, make cuts at 2-inch intervals along each long side, cutting from the edges almost to the filling. Alternately fold opposite strips of dough at an angle across the filling, lightly pressing ends together in center to seal.
4. In a small bowl whisk together egg and the water; brush loaf with egg mixture. Bake about 25 minutes or until golden.
5. Cool on baking sheet on a wire rack for 10 minutes. Drizzle with Lemon Glaze; sprinkle with almonds. Serve warm or cool completely. Chill within 2 hours.
Lemon Glaze In a small bowl stir together 1 cup powdered sugar, 1 tablespoon lemon juice, and ½ teaspoon vanilla. Add enough additional lemon juice (1 to 2 teaspoons) to reach drizzling consistency.
PER SERVING *272 cal., 9 g fat (4 g sat. fat), 48 mg chol., 253 mg sodium, 42 g carb., 2 g fiber, 8 g pro.*

LEMON-ALMOND
CREAM BREAD

CHOCOLATE-CHERRY
STRUDEL ROLLS

Puffy Linzer Claws

PREP 30 minutes
BAKE 20 minutes at 375°F
MAKES 12 servings

- 1 egg white
- 4 ounces almond paste
- ¼ cup granulated sugar
- ¼ cup packed brown sugar
- ½ teaspoon vanilla
- 1 17.3-ounce package (2 sheets) frozen puff pastry, thawed
- ½ cup seedless raspberry jam
  Water
- 1 egg white, lightly beaten
- ⅓ cup sliced almonds

1. Preheat oven to 375°F. Line a large baking sheet with parchment paper; set aside. In a medium mixing bowl beat 1 egg white and almond paste with an electric mixer on medium until combined. Add granulated sugar, brown sugar, and vanilla; beat about 1 minute or until smooth.
2. On a lightly floured surface, unfold each sheet of pastry. Roll pastry into a 12×10-inch rectangle. Cut each rectangle into six 5×4-inch rectangles. Spoon 1 rounded tablespoon of the almond mixture onto each rectangle, spreading slightly. Top each with 2 teaspoons of the jam. Moisten outside edge of pastry with water. Fold each rectangle in half lengthwise to make a 5×2-inch pastry; gently press edges to seal.
3. Place pastries on the baking sheet. Using a sharp knife or kitchen scissors, cut five ½-inch slits along the sealed side of each pastry. Curve each pastry slightly with the slits on the outside. Brush with 1 lightly beaten egg white and sprinkle with almonds.
4. Bake for 20 to 25 minutes or until golden. Cool on baking sheet on a wire rack.

PER SERVING *311 cal., 17 g fat (0 g sat. fat), 0 mg chol., 168 mg sodium, 37 g carb., 1 g fiber, 4 g pro.*

Chocolate-Cherry Strudel Rolls

PREP 20 minutes
BAKE 15 minutes at 375°F
STAND 30 minutes
MAKES 12 servings

PUFFY LINZER CLAWS

- ⅓ cup maraschino cherries, coarsely chopped
- 1 8-ounce package reduced-fat cream cheese (Neufchâtel), softened
- ¾ cup powdered sugar
- ½ teaspoon almond extract
- 2 ounces bittersweet chocolate, chopped
- 12 sheets frozen phyllo dough (14×9-inch rectangles), thawed
- ⅓ cup butter, melted
- 2 ounces bittersweet chocolate, chopped
- ½ teaspoon shortening

1. Pat cherries dry with paper towels; set aside. For filling, in a medium bowl stir together cream cheese, powdered sugar, and almond extract. Fold in cherries and 2 ounces chocolate.
2. Preheat oven to 375°F. Line a baking sheet with parchment paper; set aside. Unroll phyllo dough; cover with plastic wrap. (As you work, keep the phyllo covered to prevent it from drying out; remove sheets as you need them.) Place 1 sheet of phyllo on a work surface; brush with some of the melted butter. Top with a second sheet of phyllo. Repeat brushing and layering four more times (6 sheets total). Brush top with melted butter. Cut phyllo stack crosswise into thirds, then lengthwise in half to make six squares. Repeat with the remaining phyllo sheets and more melted butter to make 12 squares total.
3. Spoon 1 tablespoon of the filling near bottom edge of each phyllo square. Fold bottom edge of phyllo over filling; fold in sides. Roll up to enclose filling, folding in sides as you roll. Place rolls, seam sides down, on baking sheet. Brush with melted butter.
4. Bake for 15 to 17 minutes or until golden. Transfer to a wire rack; cool.
5. In a saucepan cook and stir 2 ounces chocolate and shortening over low heat until melted and smooth. Place strudel rolls on waxed paper. Drizzle with melted chocolate; let stand about 30 minutes or until chocolate is set.

PER SERVING *215 cal., 13 g fat (8 g sat. fat), 28 mg chol., 153 mg sodium, 23 g carb., 1 g fiber, 3 g pro.*

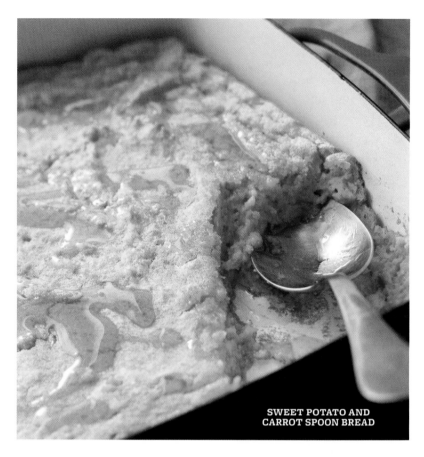

SWEET POTATO AND CARROT SPOON BREAD

Sweet Potato and Carrot Spoon Bread

PREP 20 minutes COOK 25 minutes
BAKE 40 minutes at 400°F
MAKES 10 servings

1½ pounds sweet potatoes, peeled and cut into 1-inch pieces
 1 pound carrots, peeled and cut into 1-inch pieces (about 6 medium)
 2 cups milk
 ¼ cup yellow cornmeal
 2 tablespoons butter, cut up
 2 teaspoons ground cinnamon
 ½ teaspoon salt
 ½ cup all-purpose flour
 ½ cup pure maple syrup
 ½ cup whipping cream
 4 egg yolks, lightly beaten
 4 egg whites
   Honey (optional)

1. Preheat oven to 400°F. Grease a 3-quart rectangular baking dish; set aside. In a large saucepan cook sweet potatoes and carrots in lightly salted boiling water for 20 to 25 minutes or until tender; drain and return to pot. Use a potato masher to mash the mixture until nearly smooth. Set aside.
2. In a medium saucepan combine milk, cornmeal, butter, cinnamon, and salt. Bring to boiling over medium heat, stirring constantly. Reduce heat. Simmer, uncovered, about 5 minutes or until slightly thickened. Cool slightly.
3. In a very large bowl combine mashed sweet potato mixture, cornmeal mixture, flour, maple syrup, whipping cream, and egg yolks.
4. In a medium mixing bowl beat egg whites with an electric mixer on medium to high until stiff peaks form (tips stand straight). Gently fold some of the beaten egg whites into squash mixture to lighten. Fold in remaining egg whites. Pour batter into the prepared baking dish. Bake about 40 minutes or until top is golden and center feels firm when lightly touched. Cool slightly. If desired, drizzle with honey.
PER SERVING *267 cal., 10 g fat (5 g sat. fat), 100 mg chol., 298 mg sodium, 39 g carb., 4 g fiber, 7 g pro.*

Whole Grain Sunflower Bread

PREP 20 minutes COOL 10 minutes
BAKE 45 minutes at 350°F
MAKES 14 servings

1½ cups all-purpose flour
 ¾ cup packed brown sugar
 ½ cup whole wheat flour
 ½ cup dry-roasted sunflower kernels
 ⅓ cup flaxseed meal
 1 teaspoon baking powder
 ½ teaspoon baking soda
 ½ teaspoon salt
 ½ teaspoon egg
 1 buttermilk or sour milk*
 ¼ cup vegetable oil
   Dry-roasted sunflower kernels

1. Preheat oven to 350°F. Grease the bottom and ½ inch up sides of a 9×5×3-inch loaf pan; set aside.
2. In a large bowl stir together all-purpose flour, brown sugar, whole wheat flour, the ½ cup sunflower kernels, the flaxseed meal, baking powder, baking soda, and salt. Make a well in the center of the flour mixture; set aside.
3. In a medium bowl beat egg with a fork; stir in buttermilk and oil. Add egg mixture all at once to the flour mixture. Stir just until moistened (batter should be lumpy).
4. Spoon batter into prepared pan; spread evenly. Sprinkle with additional sunflower kernels. Bake in the preheated oven for 45 to 55 minutes or until a toothpick inserted near the center comes out clean.
5. Cool in pan on a wire rack for 10 minutes. Remove from pan.
*To make 1¼ cups sour milk, place 4 teaspoons lemon juice or vinegar in a glass measuring cup. Add enough milk to make 1¼ cups total liquid; stir. Let stand for 5 minutes before using.
PER SERVING *202 cal., 8 g fat (1 g sat. fat), 16 mg chol., 207 mg sodium, 28 g carb., 2 g fiber, 5 g pro.*

CRANBERRY-PUMPKIN
GINGERBREAD WITH
SHERRY-CREAM CHEESE
DRIZZLE

Cranberry-Pumpkin Gingerbread with Sherry-Cream Cheese Drizzle

PREP 25 minutes
BAKE 55 minutes at 350°F
COOL 30 minutes   MAKES 10 servings

2 cups all-purpose flour
½ cup whole wheat flour
½ cup yellow cornmeal
1 cup sugar
2 teaspoons ground ginger
1 teaspoon ground cinnamon
1 teaspoon ground nutmeg
¼ teaspoon black pepper
¾ cup butter, cut up
1 15-ounce can pumpkin
2 eggs
½ cup full-flavor molasses
⅓ cup buttermilk
1½ teaspoons baking soda

1 cup dried cranberries
1 recipe Sherry-Cream Cheese Drizzle

1. Preheat oven to 350°F. Grease a 9-inch springform pan; place pan in a shallow baking pan. Set aside.
2. In a large bowl stir together all-purpose flour, whole wheat flour, cornmeal, sugar, ginger, cinnamon, nutmeg, and black pepper. Using a pastry blender, cut in butter until mixture forms coarse crumbs. Remove ¾ cup of crumb mixture; set aside.
3. In a medium bowl whisk together pumpkin, eggs, molasses, buttermilk, and baking soda until well combined. Add pumpkin mixture and the cranberries to remaining crumb mixture. Stir just until moistened. Spoon batter into the prepared pan. Sprinkle top of batter evenly with the reserved ¾ cup crumb mixture.

4. Bake for 55 to 60 minutes or until a long wooden skewer inserted near the center comes out clean. Cool gingerbread in pan on a wire rack for 30 minutes. Remove sides of pan.
5. Spoon Sherry-Cream Cheese Drizzle over warm gingerbread. To serve, cut gingerbread into wedges.

Sherry-Cream Cheese Drizzle In a medium mixing bowl beat one 3-ounce package cream cheese, softened, and 1 tablespoon butter, softened, with an electric mixer on medium to high until combined. Beat in ¾ cup powdered sugar, 2 tablespoons dry sherry, and ½ teaspoon vanilla until smooth. If necessary, beat in enough milk, 1 teaspoon at a time, to make a thick drizzling consistency.

PER SERVING *535 cal., 20 g fat (12 g sat. fat), 92 mg chol., 355 mg sodium, 85 g carb., 4 g fiber, 7 g pro.*

Streusel Apple Bread

(photo page 58)

PREP 30 minutes
BAKE 55 minutes at 350°F
COOL 10 minutes MAKES 12 servings

2 cups all-purpose flour
1 cup chopped apple
½ cup butter, softened
1 cup granulated sugar
2 eggs
1 teaspoon vanilla
1 teaspoon baking soda
½ teaspoon salt
⅓ cup sour milk* or orange juice
⅓ cup chopped cranberries
⅔ cup chopped walnuts
⅓ cup packed brown sugar
2 tablespoons all-purpose flour
1 teaspoon finely shredded lemon peel
1 tablespoon butter, melted

1. Preheat oven to 350°F. Grease bottom and ½ inch up sides of a 9×5×3-inch loaf pan; set aside. In a small bowl toss 2 tablespoons of the 2 cups flour with the apple; set aside. In a large mixing bowl beat ½ cup butter with an electric mixer on medium for 30 seconds; gradually beat in granulated sugar until combined. Beat in eggs and vanilla. Combine remaining flour with baking soda and salt; add to beaten mixture alternately with milk. Stir in apple mixture, cranberries, and ⅓ cup of the walnuts. Spoon into prepared pan, spreading evenly.
2. In a medium bowl combine brown sugar, 2 tablespoons flour, lemon peel, 1 tablespoon melted butter, and remaining nuts; sprinkle evenly over batter in pan. Bake, uncovered, for 55 to 60 minutes or until a toothpick inserted near the center comes out clean.
3. Cool in pan on wire rack 10 minutes. Remove from pan and cool completely on wire rack. Wrap and store overnight at room temperature before slicing.
*To make ⅓ cup sour milk, place 1 teaspoon lemon juice or vinegar in a 1 cup glass measure; add milk to equal ⅓ cup. Let stand 5 minutes.
PER SERVING 310 cal., 14 g fat (6 g sat. fat), 59 mg chol., 281 mg sodium, 43 g carb., 1 g fiber, 3 g pro.

Chai Breakfast Muffins

PREP 25 minutes
BAKE 15 minutes at 350°F
COOL 5 minutes MAKES 24 servings

1½ cups all-purpose flour
½ cup whole wheat flour
1½ teaspoons baking powder
½ teaspoon baking soda
½ teaspoon ground ginger
¼ teaspoon salt
1¼ cups milk
4 chai tea bags
½ cup butter, softened
1½ cups sugar
½ teaspoon vanilla
2 eggs
¾ cup maple-flavor granola or granola with dried fruit
1 recipe Chai Cream Cheese Icing (optional)

1. Preheat oven to 350°F. Line twenty-four 2½-inch muffin cups with paper bake cups. In a medium bowl stir together all-purpose flour, whole wheat flour, baking powder, baking soda, ginger, and salt. In a small saucepan heat milk just until simmering. Remove from heat. Add tea bags; steep for 5 minutes. Remove tea bags, pressing bags to release excess tea back into saucepan. Cool.
2. Preheat oven to 350°F. In a large mixing bowl beat butter with an electric mixer on medium to high about 1 minute or until fluffy. Add sugar and vanilla; beat until combined. Add eggs, one at a time, beating well after each addition. Alternately add flour mixture and milk mixture to butter mixture, beating on low after each addition just until combined.
3. Spoon batter into prepared muffin cups, filling each about two-thirds full. Use the back of a spoon to smooth out batter in cups. Sprinkle with granola.
4. Bake for 15 to 20 minutes or until a wooden toothpick inserted in centers comes out clean. Cool in muffin cups on wire racks for 5 minutes. Remove muffins from cups. Cool completely on wire racks. If desired, drizzle with Chai Cream Cheese Icing.
PER SERVING 181 cal., 6 g fat (3 g sat. fat), 35 mg chol., 138 mg sodium, 29 g carb., 1 g fiber, 3 g pro.

Chai-Cream Cheese Icing In a large mixing bowl combine one 3-ounce package cream cheese, softened; 2 tablespoons butter softened; and 1 teaspoon vanilla. Beat with an electric mixer on medium to high until light and fluffy. Gradually beat in 1¼ cups powdered sugar. Whisk in enough cooled brewed chai tea, 1 teaspoon at a time, to reach drizzling consistency.

Double Chocolate Muffins

PREP 15 minutes
BAKE 18 minutes at 375°F
COOL 5 minutes MAKES 12 servings

1¼ cups all-purpose flour
½ cup granulated sugar
⅓ cup packed brown sugar
¼ cup unsweetened cocoa powder
2 teaspoons baking powder
¼ teaspoon baking soda
¼ teaspoon salt
1 cup miniature semisweet chocolate pieces
½ cup vegetable oil
½ cup milk
1 egg

1. Preheat oven to 375°F. Grease twelve 2½-inch muffin cups or line with paper bake cups; set aside. In a medium bowl combine flour, granulated sugar, brown sugar, cocoa powder, baking powder, baking soda, and salt. Stir in chocolate pieces. Make a well in center of flour mixture; set aside.
2. In a small bowl whisk together the oil, milk, and egg. Add oil mixture all at once to the flour mixture. Stir just until moistened. Spoon batter into prepared muffin cups, filling each two-thirds full. Bake for 18 to 20 minutes or until edges are firm (tops will be slightly rounded). Cool in muffin cups on a wire rack for 5 minutes. Remove from muffin cups; serve warm.
PER SERVING 295 cal., 15 g fat (4 g sat. fat), 19 mg chol., 148 mg sodium, 38 g carb., 2 g fiber, 3 g pro.

DOUBLE CHOCOLATE
MUFFINS

MAPLE SWIRL BISCUITS

Maple Swirl Biscuits

PREP 35 minutes
BAKE 18 minutes at 375°F
MAKES 12 servings

- 4 cups all-purpose flour
- 4 teaspoons baking powder
- 1 teaspoon baking soda
- 1 teaspoon salt
- ½ cup cold butter
- 1¼ cups milk
- ¼ cup pure maple syrup
- ½ cup maple sugar or granulated sugar
- 1 tablespoon apple pie spice
- ½ cup butter, softened
- ⅔ cup raisins (optional)
- 2 tablespoons butter, melted
- 1 recipe Maple Glaze

1. Preheat oven to 375°F. Line a 15×10×1-inch baking pan with parchment paper, extending edges over ends of pan; set aside. In a large bowl combine flour, baking powder, baking soda, and salt. Using a pastry blender, cut in the ½ cup cold butter until mixture resembles coarse crumbs. Make a well in the center of the flour mixture.
2. Add milk and maple syrup all at once to flour mixture. Using a fork, stir just until dough forms a ball.
3. On a lightly floured surface knead dough by folding and gently pressing it for 10 to 12 strokes or just until dough holds together. If desired, place dough between two pieces of parchment paper. Roll or pat dough into a 14×10-inch rectangle.
4. In a small bowl combine maple sugar and apple pie spice. Spread dough with ½ cup softened butter; sprinkle with the sugar-spice mixture. If desired, sprinkle with raisins. Starting from a long side, roll up into a spiral. Pinch seam to seal. Using a sharp knife, cut into 12 slices. Arrange slices, cut sides down, in the prepared pan. Drizzle with the 2 tablespoons melted butter.
5. Bake for 18 to 20 minutes or until golden. Using edges of parchment paper, lift from pan to a wire rack. Cool slightly. Drizzle with Maple Glaze.
Maple Glaze In a small bowl combine 1¼ cups powdered sugar and 2 tablespoons pure maple syrup. Stir in enough milk (1 to 2 teaspoons), 1 teaspoon at a time, to make drizzling consistency.
PER SERVING *428 cal., 18 g fat (11 g sat. fat), 48 mg chol., 555 mg sodium, 62 g carb., 1 g fiber, 5 g pro.*

GINGER-PEAR SCONES

Ginger-Pear Scones

PREP 30 minutes
BAKE 8 minutes at 400°F
MAKES 30 servings

- 2½ cups all-purpose flour
- 2 tablespoons packed brown sugar
- 1 tablespoon baking powder
- 1 tablespoon finely chopped crystallized ginger
- ½ teaspoon freshly grated nutmeg or ¼ teaspoon ground nutmeg
- ¼ teaspoon salt
- ⅓ cup butter, cut up
- 1 cup finely chopped Bosc pear
- 2 eggs, lightly beaten
- ⅔ cup whipping cream
  Whipping cream
  Freshly grated nutmeg and/ or finely chopped crystallized ginger (optional)
- 1 recipe Spiced Butter

1. Preheat oven to 400°F. In a large bowl stir together flour, brown sugar, baking powder, 1 tablespoon ginger, ½ teaspoon grated or ¼ teaspoon ground nutmeg, and salt. Using a pastry blender, cut in butter until mixture resembles coarse crumbs. Stir in pear. Make a well in center of flour mixture; set aside.
2. In a medium bowl combine eggs and ⅔ cup whipping cream. Add egg mixture all at once to flour mixture. Using a fork, stir just until moistened.
3. Turn dough out onto a lightly floured surface. Knead dough by folding and gently pressing it for 10 to 12 strokes or until dough is nearly smooth. Divide dough in half. Lightly roll or pat half of the dough at a time into a 7-inch circle. Using a 2- to 2½-inch cutter, cut out scones. Reroll scraps to cut additional scones.
4. Place scones 2 inches apart on an ungreased baking sheet. Brush with additional whipping cream. If desired, sprinkle with additional grated nutmeg and/or ginger. Bake for 8 to 12 minutes or until golden. Serve warm with Spiced Butter.
Spiced Butter In a small bowl stir together 1 tablespoon sugar, ½ teaspoon finely chopped crystallized ginger, ¼ teaspoon freshly grated nutmeg or ⅛ teaspoon ground nutmeg, and dash ground cinnamon. Stir in ½ cup softened butter until combined. Cover and chill until ready to serve.
PER SERVING *119 cal., 8 g fat (5 g sat. fat), 35 mg chol., 109 mg sodium, 11 g carb., 1 g fiber, 2 g pro.*

Pure Dessert

SPECIAL SWEETS The most wonderful time of the year deserves the most wonderful desserts. Whether it's a fruit pie, indulgent chocolate cake, or an over-the-top cheesecake, you'll find the perfect ending to your holiday meal here.

ALMOND CHEESECAKE, PAGE 86

RUM-VANILLA
BEAN CAKE

flour mixture and milk mixture to butter mixture, beating on low after each addition just until combined. Pour batter into the prepared pan, spreading evenly.

3. Bake about 45 minutes or until a wooden toothpick inserted near the center comes out clean. Cool cake in pan on a wire rack for 10 minutes. Remove cake from pan; cool completely on wire rack. Sprinkle with powdered sugar.

PER SERVING *264 cal., 13 g fat (8 g sat. fat), 78 mg chol., 181 mg sodium, 31 g carb., 0 g fiber, 3 g pro.*

Carrot-Coconut Cream Cake with Raisin-Rum Filling

PREP **1 hour** STAND **30 minutes**
BAKE **30 minutes at 350°F**
CHILL **30 minutes**
MAKES **16 servings**

- 1   egg
- 1   cup all-purpose flour
- ½   teaspoon baking soda
- ½   teaspoon ground cinnamon
- ½   teaspoon ground ginger
- 1   cup finely shredded carrots
- ½   cup packed brown sugar
- ½   cup chopped walnuts, toasted (see tip, page 25)
- ½   cup vegetable oil
- ¼   cup buttermilk
- ⅓   cup butter
- 1   egg
- 1   egg white
- 1   cup all-purpose flour
- 1   teaspoon baking powder
- ⅔   cup granulated sugar
- 2   teaspoons vanilla
- 1   cup unsweetened coconut milk
- 1   cup sweetened flaked coconut
- ¼   cup dark rum
- ½   cup raisins
- ⅓   cup evaporated milk
- ¼   cup packed brown sugar
- 3   tablespoons butter
- 1   egg yolk
- ¾   cup sweetened flaked coconut
- ⅓   cup chopped walnuts, toasted (see tip, page 25)
- ½   teaspoon vanilla
- 1   recipe Cream Cheese Frosting

Rum-Vanilla Bean Cake

PREP **25 minutes** STAND **30 minutes**
BAKE **45 minutes at 325°F**
COOL **10 minutes** MAKES **12 servings**

- ¾   cup butter
- 2   eggs
- 1   egg yolk
- 1½ cups all-purpose flour
- 2   teaspoons baking powder
- ½   cup milk
- ¼   cup light rum
- 2   vanilla beans, split lengthwise
- ¾   cup granulated sugar
- ¼   cup packed brown sugar
       Powdered sugar

1. Allow butter, eggs, and egg yolk to stand at room temperature for 30 minutes. Meanwhile, generously grease and lightly flour a 10-inch fluted tube pan; set aside. In a small bowl stir together flour and baking powder. In a medium bowl combine milk and rum. Using the tip of a small sharp knife, scrape out seeds from vanilla beans. Stir vanilla seeds into milk mixture; set aside.

2. Preheat oven to 325°F. In a large mixing bowl beat butter with an electric mixer on medium to high for 30 seconds. Gradually add granulated sugar and brown sugar, beating about 10 minutes or until light and fluffy. Add eggs and egg yolk; beat for 1 minute. Alternately add

**CARROT-COCONUT
CREAM CAKE WITH
RAISIN-RUM FILLING**

Chopped walnuts, toasted (see
tip, page 25)
Shaved coconut, toasted (see tip,
page 25) (optional)

1. Allow eggs, butter, and egg
white for cake layers to stand at
room temperature for 30 minutes.
Meanwhile, preheat oven to 350°F.
Grease and flour two 8×1½-inch round
cake pans; set aside.
2. For the carrot cake layer, in a large
bowl stir together flour, baking soda,
cinnamon, and ginger; set aside.
In a medium bowl combine egg,
carrots, brown sugar, walnuts, oil,
and buttermilk. Add egg mixture to
flour mixture; stir until combined.
Pour batter into one of the prepared
pans, spreading evenly. Bake for
22 to 25 minutes or until a wooden
toothpick inserted near the center
comes out clean.
3. For the coconut cake layer, in a
small bowl stir together flour and
baking powder; set aside. In a large
mixing bowl beat butter with an
electric mixer on medium to high for
30 seconds. Add granulated sugar and
vanilla. Beat until combined, scraping
sides of bowl occasionally. Add egg and
egg white; beat just until combined.
Alternately add flour mixture and
coconut milk to butter mixture,
beating on low after each addition just
until combined. Stir in coconut. Pour
batter into the remaining prepared
pan, spreading evenly. Bake alongside
carrot cake layer for 30 to 35 minutes
or until a wooden toothpick inserted
near the center comes out clean.
4. Cool cake layers in pans on wire racks
for 10 minutes. Remove layers from
pans; cool completely on wire racks.
5. Meanwhile, for raisin-rum filling,
in a small saucepan bring rum just
to boiling over medium-high heat.
Remove from heat. Stir in raisins.
Let stand, covered, for 5 minutes.
Drain, discarding rum. Set raisins
aside. In the same saucepan combine
evaporated milk, brown sugar,
butter, and egg yolk. Cook and stir
over medium heat until thickened
and bubbly (165°F). Stir in raisins,
coconut, walnuts, and vanilla; cool.
Cover and chill until needed.
6. To assemble, place carrot cake layer,
bottom (flat) side up, on a serving
platter. Spread with raisin-rum filling.
Top with coconut cake layer, top
(rounded) side up. Spread top and
sides with Cream Cheese Frosting.
Sprinkle with toasted walnuts and,
if desired, toasted coconut. Chill for
30 minutes before serving.
Cream Cheese Frosting Allow
two 3-ounce packages cream cheese
and ½ cup butter to stand at room
temperature for 30 minutes. In a large
mixing bowl beat cream cheese, butter,
and 1 teaspoon vanilla with an electric
mixer on medium until light and fluffy.
Gradually beat in 4 cups powdered
sugar to reach spreading consistency.
PER SERVING *648 cal., 37 g fat (18 g sat.
fat), 79 mg chol., 268 mg sodium, 73 g carb.,
2 g fiber, 7 g pro.*

Chocolate-Espresso Chiffon Cake

PREP **1 hour 5 minutes**
BAKE **1 hour at 325°F**
MAKES **14 servings**

8 eggs
4 teaspoons espresso powder or instant coffee crystals
¾ cup water
2 cups all-purpose flour
1½ cups sugar
1 tablespoon baking powder
1 teaspoon salt
½ cup cooking oil
1 teaspoon vanilla
3 ounces bittersweet chocolate, grated
½ teaspoon cream of tartar
1 recipe Espresso Whipped Cream
Grated chocolate (optional)

1. Separate eggs, discarding 3 of the yolks or saving for another use. Let eggs stand at room temperature 30 minutes. Preheat oven to 325°F. Dissolve espresso in the water.

CHOCOLATE-ESPRESSO CHIFFON CAKE

2. In a large bowl stir together flour, sugar, baking powder, and salt; make well in center. Add oil, the 5 egg yolks, dissolved espresso, and vanilla. Beat on low until moistened; beat on medium-high 4 to 5 minutes or until satin-smooth. Stir in grated chocolate.
3. Wash and dry beaters. In a 4-quart bowl beat egg whites and cream of tartar on medium-high until stiff peaks form (tips stand straight). Pour chocolate batter in thin stream over surface of whites; fold to blend. Spoon into an ungreased 10-inch tube pan.
4. Bake 60 to 70 minutes or until top springs back when lightly touched near center. Invert pan to cool. Carefully loosen sides; remove from pan. Serve with Espresso Whipped Cream and, if desired, sprinkle with grated chocolate.

Espresso Whipped Cream In a chilled mixing bowl combine 1 cup whipping cream, 1 tablespoon sugar, ½ to 1 teaspoon espresso powder or instant coffee crystals, and ½ teaspoon vanilla. Beat with an electric mixer on medium until soft peaks form (tips curl).

PER SERVING *354 cal., 19 g fat (7 g sat. fat), 99 mg chol., 286 mg sodium, 42 g carb., 1 g fiber, 4 g pro.*

Dark Cocoa Buttermilk Cake with Cocoa Mascarpone Frosting

PREP **30 minutes**
BAKE **30 minutes at 350°F**
COOL **10 minutes**
MAKES **12 servings**

¾ cup butter
3 eggs
2⅓ cups all-purpose flour
¾ cup Dutch-process unsweetened cocoa powder or unsweetened cocoa powder
1 teaspoon baking soda
¾ teaspoon baking powder
½ teaspoon salt
1 cup granulated sugar
1 cup packed brown sugar
2 teaspoons vanilla
1½ cups buttermilk
1 recipe Cocoa Mascarpone Frosting
White and dark chocolate shavings (optional)

1. Allow butter and eggs to stand at room temperature for 30 minutes. Meanwhile, lightly grease bottoms of three 8×1½-inch round cake pans. Line bottoms of pans with waxed paper. Grease and lightly flour bottoms and sides of pans. Set pans aside. Preheat oven to 350°F.
2. In a medium mixing bowl stir together the flour, cocoa powder, baking soda, baking powder and salt.
3. In a large mixing bowl beat butter with an electric mixer on medium to high for 30 seconds. In a small bowl combine granulated and brown sugars. Gradually add sugar mixture, about ¼ cup at a time, beating on medium until well combined (3 to 4 minutes). Scrape sides of bowl; continue beating on medium for 2 minutes. Add eggs, one at a time, beating well after each addition. Beat in vanilla.
4. Add flour mixture and buttermilk alternately to beaten mixture, beating on low just until combined after each addition. Beat on medium to high for 20 seconds more. Spread batter evenly into the prepared pans.
5. Bake for 30 to 35 minutes or until a wooden toothpick inserted in the centers comes out clean. Cool cake layers in pans for 10 minutes on wire rack. Remove from pans. Peel off waxed paper. Cool thoroughly on wire racks.
6. To assemble, place a cake layer on a cake plate. Spread with ½ cup of the Cocoa Mascarpone Frosting. Top with second cake layer; spread with another ½ cup of the frosting. Top with the remaining cake layer. Frost top and sides with remaining frosting. If desired, top with chocolate shavings. Cover and store in the refrigerator.

Cocoa Mascarpone Frosting In a large mixing bowl beat 4 ounces softened mascarpone cheese or cream cheese, ½ cup softened butter, ⅓ cup unsweetened dark Dutch-process cocoa powder or unsweetened cocoa powder, 2 tablespoons milk, and 2 teaspoons vanilla with an electric mixer on medium to high until creamy. Gradually add 1 pound powdered sugar, beating until smooth. Beat in additional milk, 1 teaspoon at a time, to reach spreading consistency.

PER SERVING *633 cal., 26 g fat (16 g sat. fat), 117 mg chol., 419 mg sodium, 98 g carb., 3 g fiber, 9 g pro.*

Looking for a dessert with a wow factor? How about a triple-layer chocolate buttermilk cake with silky frosting and chocolate curls?

DARK COCOA BUTTERMILK
CAKE WITH COCOA
MASCARPONE FROSTING

GOOEY CHOCOLATE
PUDDING CAKES

Gooey Chocolate Pudding Cakes

PREP 20 minutes
BAKE 20 minutes at 350°F
MAKES 6 servings

- ½ cup all-purpose flour
- ¼ cup sugar
- ¾ teaspoon baking powder
- ¼ teaspoon salt
- ⅓ cup milk
- 1 tablespoon oil
- 1 teaspoon vanilla
- ¼ cup chocolate-hazelnut spread (Nutella)
- ⅓ cup semisweet chocolate pieces
- ½ cup sugar
- ¼ cup unsweetened cocoa powder
- ¾ cup boiling water
  Coffee-flavor or vanilla ice cream (optional)
  Sliced strawberries (optional)
  Unsweetened cocoa powder (optional)

1. Preheat oven to 350°F. In a medium bowl combine flour, the ¼ cup sugar, baking powder, and salt. Add milk, oil, and vanilla. Whisk until smooth. Stir in chocolate-hazelnut spread and chocolate pieces.
2. Divide batter evenly among six 5- to 8-ounce oven-safe bowls or ramekins. Place in a 15×10×1-inch baking pan. Set aside. In the same bowl for the batter stir together ½ cup sugar and cocoa. Gradually stir in the boiling water. Pour evenly over batter in dishes.
3. Bake, uncovered, for 20 minutes or until a wooden toothpick inserted into cake portion comes out clean. If desired, serve warm with ice cream, strawberries and sprinkled with additional cocoa powder.

PER SERVING 272 cal., 9 g fat (2 g sat. fat), 1 mg chol., 178 mg sodium, 49 g carb., 2 g fiber, 3 g pro.

Red Velvet Cupcakes

PREP 40 minutes STAND 30 minutes
BAKE 20 minutes at 350°F
COOL 45 minutes MAKES 26 servings

- ¾ cup butter
- 3 eggs
- 3 cups all-purpose flour
- 1 tablespoon unsweetened cocoa powder

RED VELVET CUPCAKES

- ¾ teaspoon salt
- 2¼ cups sugar
- 1 1-ounce bottle red food coloring (2 tablespoons)
- 2 tablespoons raspberry liqueur or milk
- 1 teaspoon vanilla
- 1⅓ cups buttermilk or sour milk*
- 1½ teaspoons baking soda
- 1½ teaspoons vinegar
- 1 recipe Cream Cheese-Raspberry Frosting
  Fresh raspberries (optional)

1. Allow butter and eggs to stand at room temperature for 30 minutes. Meanwhile, line twenty-six 2½-inch muffin cups with paper bake cups or parchment paper. In a medium bowl stir together flour, cocoa powder, and salt. Set aside.
2. Preheat oven to 350°F. In a very large mixing bowl beat butter with an electric mixer on medium to high for 30 seconds. Gradually add sugar, about ¼ cup at a time, beating on medium until combined. Scrape sides of bowl; beat on medium about 2 minutes more or until light and fluffy. Add eggs, one at a time, beating well after each addition. Beat in red food coloring, liqueur, and vanilla. Alternately add flour mixture and buttermilk to butter mixture, beating on low after each addition just until combined. In a small bowl combine baking soda and vinegar; fold into batter.

3. Spoon batter into prepared muffin cups, filling each about three-fourths full. Use the back of a spoon to smooth out batter in cups.
4. Bake about 20 minutes or until tops spring back when lightly touched. Cool cupcakes in muffin cups on wire racks for 5 minutes. Remove cupcakes from muffin cups. Cool completely on wire racks.
5. Spread cupcakes with Cream Cheese-Raspberry Frosting. If desired top with fresh raspberries.

Cream Cheese-Raspberry Frosting
Allow half of an 8-ounce package cream cheese and ⅓ cup butter to stand at room temperature for 30 minutes. In a large mixing bowl beat cream cheese, butter, 2 tablespoons raspberry liqueur or milk, and 1 teaspoon vanilla with an electric mixer on medium until light and fluffy. Gradually beat in 4 cups powdered sugar. If necessary, beat in 1 to 3 teaspoons milk, 1 teaspoon at a time, until frosting reaches spreading consistency.
*To make 1⅓ cups sour milk, place 4 teaspoons lemon juice or vinegar in a glass measuring cup. Add enough milk to make 1⅓ cups total liquid; stir. Let stand for 5 minutes before using.

PER SERVING 298 cal., 10 g fat (6 g sat. fat), 50 mg chol., 230 mg sodium, 49 g carb., 0 g fiber, 3 g pro.

Pear-Walnut Streusel Pie

PREP 30 minutes CHILL 15 minutes
BAKE 50 minutes at 375°F
COOL 1 hour MAKES 8 servings

- 1 recipe Pastry for a Single-Crust Pie
- 6 cups thinly sliced, peeled ripe Anjou or Bosc pears (6 medium)
- ¾ cup all-purpose flour
- ¼ cup granulated sugar
- ¼ teaspoon ground cinnamon
- ¼ teaspoon ground nutmeg
- ½ cup walnuts, toasted and coarsely chopped (see tip, page 25)
- ¼ cup packed brown sugar
- ½ teaspoon ground cinnamon
- ¼ cup butter, melted
  Vanilla ice cream (optional)
  Ground cinnamon (optional)

1. Preheat oven to 375°F. Prepare Pastry for a Single-Crust Pie.
2. In a large bowl combine pears, ¼ cup of the flour, the granulated sugar, ¼ teaspoon cinnamon, and nutmeg; toss gently to coat.
3. For streusel, in a bowl stir together the remaining ½ cup flour, walnuts, brown sugar, and ½ teaspoon cinnamon. Drizzle with melted butter; toss with a fork until combined.

PEAR-WALNUT STREUSEL PIE

4. Transfer pear mixture to pastry-lined pie plate. Sprinkle with streusel. Chill for 15 minutes before baking.
5. Cover edge of pie loosely with foil. Bake for 25 minutes. Remove foil. Bake for 25 to 30 minutes or until pears are juicy and tender and streusel is golden. Cool on a wire rack about 1 hour to serve warm or cool completely. If desired, serve with ice cream and sprinkle with additional cinnamon.
Pastry for a Single-Crust Pie In a medium bowl stir together 1½ cups all-purpose flour and ½ teaspoon salt. Using a pastry blender, cut in ¼ cup shortening and ¼ cup butter, cut up, until pieces are pea size. Sprinkle 1 tablespoon ice water over part of the flour mixture; toss gently with a fork. Push moistened pastry to side of bowl. Repeat moistening flour mixture, using 1 tablespoon ice water at a time, until all of the flour mixture is moistened (¼ to ⅓ cup ice water total). Gather flour mixture into a ball, kneading gently until it holds together. On a lightly floured surface use your hands to slightly flatten pastry. Roll pastry from center edges into a circle about 12 inches in diameter. Wrap pastry circle around the rolling pin. Unroll into a 9-inch pie plate. Ease into pie plate with out stretching it. Trim pastry to ½ inch beyond edge of pie plate. Fold under extra pastry even with the plate's edge. Crimp edge as desired. Do not prick pastry.

PER SERVING *456 cal., 23 g fat (9 g sat. fat), 31 mg chol., 251 mg sodium, 60 g carb., 5 g fiber, 5 g pro.*

Butternut Squash Pie with Gingersnap Crust

PREP 40 minutes
BAKE 45 minutes at 400°F,
4 minutes at 375°F, 45 minutes at 325°F MAKES 8 servings

- 1 2-pound butternut squash
- 1¼ cups finely crushed gingersnap cookies
- ⅓ cup butter, melted
- 3 eggs, lightly beaten
- 1 14-ounce can sweetened condensed milk
- ¼ cup sugar
- 3 tablespoons butter, melted and cooled
- 1 tablespoon all-purpose flour
- ½ teaspoon ground nutmeg
- ½ teaspoon ground cinnamon
- ½ teaspoon ground ginger
- ¼ teaspoon ground cloves
  Dash salt
  Sweetened Whipped Cream (recipe, page 40) (optional)
  Ground nutmeg (optional)

1. Preheat oven to 400°F. Line a 15×10×1-inch baking pan with foil; set aside. Cut squash in half lengthwise; remove and discard seeds. Place squash halves, cut sides down, in the prepared baking pan. Bake for 45 to 60 minutes or until tender. Remove from oven. Reduce oven temperature to 375°F.
2. Scoop squash pulp from shells and place in a bowl. Mash with a potato masher. Measure 1½ cups of the mashed squash; set aside. (Discard the remaining pulp or save for another use.)
3. For crust, in a medium bowl toss together crushed gingersnaps and ⅓ cup melted butter. Press mixture onto the bottom and up the sides of a 9-inch pie plate. Bake for 4 to 5 minutes or until edges are light brown. Remove from oven. Reduce oven temperature to 325°F.
4. In a large bowl combine eggs, condensed milk, sugar, and 3 tablespoons melted butter. Stir in mashed squash. In a small bowl stir together flour, nutmeg, cinnamon, ginger, cloves, and salt. Stir flour mixture into squash mixture just until combined.
5. Place crust-lined pie plate in a 15×10×1-inch baking pan. Carefully pour squash mixture into crust. Bake about 45 minutes or just until filling is set. Cool on a wire rack. If desired serve with Sweetened Whipped Cream and sprinkle with nutmeg. Cover and chill pie within 2 hours.

PER SERVING *445 cal., 20 g fat (11 g sat. fat), 118 mg chol., 316 mg sodium, 61 g carb., 3 g fiber, 9 g pro.*

BUTTERNUT SQUASH
PIE WITH GINGERSNAP
CRUST

ITALIAN SILK PIE

Italian Silk Pie

PREP 45 minutes
BAKE 5 minutes at 375°F
CHILL 2 hours
MAKES 10 servings

- 6 tablespoons butter
- 1 ounce semisweet chocolate, chopped
- 1¼ cups finely crushed chocolate wafer cookies
- ¼ cup ground almonds
- 2 tablespoons granulated sugar
- 4 ounces semisweet chocolate, coarsely chopped
- 1 tablespoon amaretto
- 2 teaspoons instant espresso coffee powder
- 4 ounces cream cheese, softened
- 6 tablespoons powdered sugar
- 1 8-ounce carton mascarpone cheese, softened
- 1 teaspoon vanilla
- 1½ cups whipping cream
- 2 teaspoons amaretto
  Chocolate shavings (optional)

1. Preheat oven to 375°F. In a small saucepan cook and stir butter and 1 ounce chocolate over low heat until melted. Cool to room temperature.
2. For crust, in a bowl stir together crushed cookies, ground almonds, and granulated sugar. Stir in butter mixture until combined. Press mixture onto the bottom and up the sides of a 9-inch pie plate. Bake for 5 to 8 minutes or until set. Cool on a wire rack.
3. Meanwhile, place 4 ounces chocolate in a small microwave-safe bowl. Heat on high for 40 to 60 seconds or until melted and smooth, stirring twice; set aside.
4. In another small bowl stir together 1 tablespoon amaretto and espresso powder until powder is dissolved.
5. In a large mixing bowl beat cream cheese with an electric mixer on medium until smooth. Beat in 4 tablespoons (¼ cup) of the powdered sugar. Beat in mascarpone cheese just until combined. Using a rubber spatula, fold in melted chocolate, amaretto mixture, and vanilla just until combined (do not overmix).
6. In a medium mixing bowl beat whipping cream on medium until soft peaks form (tips curl). Add the

remaining 2 tablespoons powdered sugar and 2 teaspoons amaretto. Beat just until stiff peaks begin to form. Fold about one-fourth of the whipped cream into chocolate mixture. Pour mixture into piecrust, spreading evenly. Pipe or spread remaining whipped cream over chocolate mixture. Chill pie for 2 to 12 hours before serving. If desired sprinkle with chocolate shavings.

PER SERVING 504 cal., 42 g fat (24 g sat. fat), 109 mg chol., 223 mg sodium, 31 g carb., 2 g fiber, 8 g pro.

Brown-Bottom Butterscotch Cashew Cream Pie

PREP 50 minutes
BAKE 23 minutes at 350°F
COOL 1 hour CHILL 4 hours
MAKES 8 servings

- 1¼ cups finely crushed graham crackers (21 squares)
- 1 cup roasted salted cashews
- ⅓ cup granulated sugar
- ½ cup butter, melted
- ⅔ cup whipping cream
- 1 cup semisweet chocolate pieces
- ¾ cup packed brown sugar
- ¼ cup cornstarch
- ¼ teaspoon salt
- 1 12-ounce can evaporated milk
- 3 egg yolks
- 1 cup milk
- 3 tablespoons butter
- 1 teaspoon vanilla
- 1 recipe Brown Sugar Meringue

1. Preheat oven to 350°F. In a food processor combine crushed crackers, cashews, and granulated sugar. Cover and pulse with several on/off turns to form fine crumbs. Add the melted butter; cover and pulse with several on/off turns to combine. Press mixture onto the bottom and up the sides of a 9-inch pie plate. Bake for 8 to 10 minutes or until fragrant and firm. Cool on a wire rack.
2. In a small saucepan bring whipping cream just to boiling over medium-high heat. Remove from heat; add chocolate pieces (do not stir). Let stand 5 minutes. Stir until smooth. Pour chocolate mixture evenly over the bottom of the crust.

3. For filling, in a medium saucepan combine brown sugar, cornstarch, and salt. Whisk in about ½ cup of the evaporated milk. Whisk in egg yolks until combined. Whisk in the remaining evaporated milk and the milk. Cook and stir over medium heat until thickened and bubbly. Remove from heat. Stir in the 3 tablespoons butter and the vanilla. Cover and keep warm.
4. Prepare Brown Sugar Meringue. Pour warm filling into prepared piecrust. Spread meringue over warm filling, sealing to edge of crust and swirling meringue into peaks. Bake for 15 minutes or until meringue is firm and golden. Cool on a wire rack for 1 hour. Chill for 4 to 6 hours before serving; cover for longer storage.
Brown Sugar Meringue Let 4 egg whites stand at room temperature for 30 minutes. In a large mixing bowl beat egg whites with an electric mixer on medium until soft peaks form (tips curl). Gradually add ¼ cup packed brown sugar and ¼ cup granulated sugar, 1 tablespoon at a time, beating on high until stiff peaks form (tips stand straight) and sugar dissolves.

PER SERVING 768 cal., 45 g fat (23 g sat. fat), 163 mg chol., 512 mg sodium, 85 g carb., 2 g fiber, 12 g pro.

BROWN-BOTTOM BUTTERSCOTCH CASHEW CREAM PIE

ALMOND CHEESECAKE

Almond Cheesecake

PREP 25 minutes
BAKE 10 minutes at 350°F/
75 minutes at 325°F COOL 3 hours
CHILL 4 hours MAKES 16 servings

1 9-ounce box chocolate wafer cookies, broken into pieces
1½ cups sliced almonds, toasted (see tip, page 25)
½ cup unsalted butter, melted
1 tablespoon sugar
¼ teaspoon salt
4 8-ounce packages cream cheese, softened
1 cup sugar
¼ teaspoon salt
1½ teaspoons vanilla
½ teaspoon almond extract
4 eggs
1 cup sour cream
¾ cup sweetened flaked coconut, toasted (see tip, page 25)

1 cup semisweet chocolate pieces (6 ounces)
¾ cup whipping cream
1½ teaspoons vanilla
¼ cup shaved fresh coconut or sweetened flaked coconut, toasted

1. Preheat oven to 350°F. For crust, in a food processor combine cookies and ½ cup of the almonds. Cover and process with on/off pulses until finely chopped. Add melted butter, 1 tablespoon sugar, and ¼ teaspoon salt. Cover and process just until combined.
2. Press almond mixture onto the bottom and about 1 inch up the sides of a 9-inch springform pan that has a removable bottom. Bake for 10 minutes. Cool on a wire rack. Reduce oven temperature to 325°F.
3. In a large mixing bowl beat cream cheese with an electric mixer on medium until smooth. Add 1 cup sugar

and ¼ teaspoon salt. Beat until light and creamy, scraping sides of bowl occasionally. Beat in 1½ teaspoons vanilla and almond extract.
4. Add eggs, one at a time, beating well after each addition. Beat in sour cream on low just until combined. Fold in ¾ cup of the almonds and ¾ cup coconut.
5. Pour cream cheese mixture into crust-lined pan, spreading evenly. Bake about 75 minutes or until a 2½-inch area around outside edge appears set when gently shaken. Cool in pan on a wire rack for 3 hours.
6. For ganache, in a small saucepan combine chocolate, whipping cream, and 1½ teaspoons vanilla. Cook and stir over medium-low heat until chocolate is melted and smooth. Cool about 20 minutes or until ganache begins to thicken but can still be poured. Using a small sharp knife, loosen crust from sides of pan. Remove sides of pan. Spread ganache over top of cheesecake.
7. Chill for 4 hours. Garnish with ¼ cup of the almonds and ¼ cup coconut.
PER SERVING *584 cal., 45 g fat (23 g sat. fat), 146 mg chol., 424 mg sodium, 41 g carb., 3 g fiber, 9 g pro.*

Bittersweet Cheesecake Torte

PREP 45 minutes
BAKE 1 hour 25 minutes at 350°F
COOL 55 minutes CHILL overnight
MAKES 12 servings

⅔ cup whipping cream
8 ounces milk chocolate or bittersweet chocolate, chopped
Nonstick spray for baking
1 19.5-ounce package brownie mix
2 8-ounce packages cream cheese, softened
½ cup sugar
2 teaspoons vanilla
2 eggs, lightly beaten
3 ounces milk chocolate or bittersweet chocolate, melted
3 ounces white baking chocolate, melted
1 recipe Candied Citrus

BITTERSWEET
CHEESECAKE
TORTE

1. In a small saucepan heat whipping cream over medium-high heat just until boiling. Remove from heat. Add the 8 ounces milk chocolate (do not stir). Let stand for 5 minutes. Stir until smooth. Transfer to a large bowl. Cover and chill.

2. Preheat oven to 350°F. Coat two 9×1½-inch round cake pans with nonstick spray for baking and line the bottom with a waxed paper circle. Prepare brownie batter according to package directions. Divide batter between prepared pans. Bake about 25 minutes or until edges are set. Cool in pans on wire racks for 10 minutes. Remove uncut brownies from pans. Transfer to a wire rack. Cool completely.

3. In a large bowl combine cream cheese, sugar, and vanilla; beat with an electric mixer on medium until combined. Beat in eggs just until combined. Transfer half of the mixture (about 1½ cups) to a medium bowl. To one bowl add the 3 ounces melted milk chocolate; stir until smooth. To the other bowl add the melted white chocolate; stir until smooth.

4. Wrap heavy-duty foil around the bottom of an 8-inch springform pan, making sure foil comes at least 1 inch up the side. Using a sharp knife, trim edges from brownie rounds, making two 8-inch rounds.* Place one of the brownie rounds in the pan. Pour milk chocolate-cream cheese mixture on top. Place the remaining brownie round on the milk chocolate-cream cheese mixture and pour white chocolate-cream cheese mixture on top.

5. Place the foil-wrapped springform pan in a large roasting pan; pour enough hot water around the springform pan to come halfway up the side. Bake for 60 to 65 minutes or until cheesecake appears set when gently shaken. Carefully remove springform pan from water.

6. Cool in springform pan on a wire rack for 15 minutes. Using a small sharp knife, loosen the edge from the side of the pan; cool for 30 minutes more. Remove the side of the pan; cool completely on wire rack. Cover and chill overnight.

7. Remove ganache from refrigerator. Beat with an electric mixer on medium until light, fluffy, and spreading consistency. Quickly spread the ganache on the top of the chilled cheesecake. Top with candied fruit.
*Before wrapping the springform pan in foil, place the bottom of the pan on each brownie round and use the tip of a sharp knife to trace around the pan bottom. Trim edges.

Candied Citrus Cut 1 clementine and 1 blood orange into ⅛-inch slices and 3 kumquats in half. Remove any seeds; set fruit aside. In a medium saucepan combine 1½ cups sugar and 1½ cups water. Cook and stir over medium-high heat until mixture begins to simmer and is clear. Reduce heat to medium. Add fruit; simmer for 15 to 20 minutes or until slices are softened, stirring occasionally. Remove from heat; cool. Drain fruit on a wire rack; if necessary, part dry with paper towels.

PER SERVING *580 cal., 36 g fat (16 g sat. fat), 126 mg chol., 302 mg sodium, 61 g carb., 2 g fiber, 8 g pro.*

**OATMEAL-BUTTERSCOTCH
COOKIE CHEESECAKE**

Oatmeal-Butterscotch Cookie Cheesecake

PREP 25 minutes   STAND 30 minutes
BAKE 45 minutes at 350°F
COOL 2 hours   CHILL 4 hours
MAKES 12 servings

- 3 8-ounce packages cream cheese
- 3 eggs, lightly beaten
- 2 cups rolled oats
- ½ cup broken pecans
- 2 tablespoons packed brown sugar
- ½ teaspoon ground cinnamon
- ½ cup butter, melted
- ½ cup granulated sugar
- ½ cup packed brown sugar
- 2 tablespoons all-purpose flour
- 1 teaspoon vanilla
- ½ teaspoon finely shredded orange peel (optional)
- ¼ cup milk
- 1¼ cups butterscotch-flavor pieces

1. Allow cream cheese and eggs to stand at room temperature for 30 minutes. Meanwhile, preheat oven to 350°F. For crust, in a food processor combine oats, pecans, 2 tablespoons brown sugar, and cinnamon. Cover and process with on/off pulses until oats and nuts are finely chopped. Add melted butter; cover and process with on/off pulses just until combined. Remove ¼ cup of the oat mixture; set aside. Press the remaining oat mixture onto the bottom and about 1 inch up the sides of a 9-inch springform pan.
2. In a large mixing bowl beat cream cheese, granulated sugar, ½ cup brown sugar, flour, vanilla, and, if desired, orange peel with an electric mixer on medium until combined. Beat in milk until smooth. Stir in eggs and 1 cup of the butterscotch pieces.
3. Pour cream cheese mixture into crust-lined pan, spreading evenly. Sprinkle the reserved oat mixture and the remaining ¼ cup butterscotch pieces around outside edge. Place springform pan in a shallow baking pan.
4. Bake for 45 to 50 minutes or until a 2½-inch area around outside edge appears set when gently shaken. Cool in springform pan on a wire rack for 15 minutes. Using a small sharp knife, loosen crust from sides of pan. Cool for 30 minutes more. Remove sides of pan; cool cheesecake completely on wire rack. Cover and chill for at least 4 hours before serving.

PER SERVING *580 cal., 39 g fat (23 g sat. fat), 130 mg chol., 291 mg sodium, 50 g carb., 2 g fiber, 8 g pro.*

Bread Pudding with Cinnamon-Pecan Syrup

PREP 50 minutes   COOL 30 minutes
BAKE 25 minutes at 350°F
MAKES 8 servings

- 1 cup water
- 1 cup granulated sugar
- 6 ounces piloncillo or 1 cup brown sugar
- 1 teaspoon finely shredded lemon peel
- 4 sticks canella or other cinnamon
- 2 whole cloves
- ⅓ cup raisins
- ½ cup pecans or slivered almonds Vegetable oil
- 4 egg whites
- 2 egg yolks
- 1½ cups milk
- 2 tablespoons granulated sugar
- 2 tablespoons dark rum or cream sherry (optional)
- 1 teaspoon vanilla
- 1 8-ounce baguette, cut into ½-inch-thick slices

1. For the cinnamon-pecan syrup, in a medium saucepan combine the water, the 1 cup granulated sugar, the piloncillo, lemon peel, cinnamon, and cloves. Bring mixture to boiling over high heat; reduce heat to medium and simmer, uncovered, until sugars are dissolved and mixture is thickened and syrupy, stirring frequently. Cool for 15 minutes. Strain to remove cinnamon and cloves. Stir in raisins and nuts; set aside (mixture will continue to thicken).
2. Meanwhile, heat ½ inch oil in a heavy large skillet to 350°F. In a large bowl beat egg whites with an electric mixer on medium-high until stiff but not dry. In another bowl whisk yolks until light and frothy, about 1 minute. Gently fold egg yolks into egg whites.
3. In a large bowl combine milk, the 2 tablespoons granulated sugar, the rum, and vanilla; stir to dissolve sugar. Dip 1 bread slice into milk mixture, turning to coat all sides and shaking gently over bowl to remove excess liquid. Dip the bread slice into the egg mixture to coat well, then transfer to the hot skillet; fry bread for 1 minute per side until lightly browned. Transfer fried bread to paper towels. Repeat with remaining bread and coatings, cooking about one-third of the slices at a time and reheating oil between batches.
4. Preheat oven to 350°F. Line the bottom of a 2-quart rectangular baking dish with half of the bread slices. Spoon half of the syrup on top. Repeat with remaining bread slices and syrup. Bake 25 to 30 minutes or until syrup bubbles and begins to caramelize. Allow to cool for 15 minutes before serving.

PER SERVING *475 cal., 15 g fat (2 g sat. fat), 29 mg chol., 248 mg sodium, 81 g carb., 0 g fiber, 7 g pro.*

BREAD PUDDING WITH
CINNAMON-PECAN SYRUP

BAKED ALASKA WITH RUM PUDDING ICE CREAM

Baked Alaska with Rum Pudding Ice Cream

PREP 30 minutes FREEZE 4 hours
BROIL 2 minutes MAKES 10 servings

Vegetable oil
¾ cup dark rum or orange juice
½ cup raisins
½ cup dried cranberries
1½ quarts vanilla ice cream
4 ounces dark chocolate
   (70% cocoa), coarsely chopped
½ teaspoon ground cinnamon
½ teaspoon ground cloves
2 tablespoons dark rum or orange juice
2 tablespoons water
1 tablespoon sugar
1 tablespoon butter, melted
1 10.75-ounce frozen pound cake, thawed
⅓ cup dried egg whites,* such as Just Whites
⅓ cup warm water
⅓ cup sugar

1. Brush a 3-quart metal bowl with oil. Line bowl with plastic wrap, extending the wrap over edges of bowl; set aside.
2. In a small saucepan combine the ¾ cup rum, raisins, and dried cranberries. Bring to boiling; reduce heat. Simmer, uncovered, for 5 minutes. Drain and let cool.
3. In a large bowl stir ice cream with a wooden spoon just until softened. Stir in raisin mixture, chocolate, cinnamon, and cloves. In a small bowl stir together 2 tablespoons rum, 2 tablespoons water, 1 tablespoon sugar, and melted butter. Cut pound cake into ½-inch slices. Brush cake slices with rum mixture.
4. Pour half of the ice cream mixture into the prepared 3-quart bowl, spreading evenly. Layer half of the cake slices on top of ice cream layer, trimming cake as necessary to fit. Top with the remaining ice cream mixture and the remaining cake slices; gently press cake into ice cream. Cover with plastic wrap. Freeze for 4 to 24 hours or until firm.
5. Adjust baking rack to the lowest position in oven. Preheat broiler. Line a pizza pan or baking sheet with foil; set aside. For meringue, in a medium mixing bowl combine dried egg whites and the warm water. Beat with an electric mixer on medium to high until soft peaks form (tips curl). Gradually add ⅓ cup sugar, beating until stiff peaks form (tips stand straight).
6. Remove plastic wrap from cake. Carefully invert cake and ice cream onto the prepared pan; remove plastic wrap. Quickly spread meringue over cake and ice cream. Using the back of a spoon, add high peaks to the meringue. Broil on the lowest rack for 2 to 4 minutes or just until meringue peaks are golden. Serve immediately.
*Look for dried egg whites in the baking section of your supermarket.
PER SERVING 503 cal., 23 g fat (13 g sat. fat), 86 mg chol., 173 mg sodium, 59 g carb., 3 g fiber, 6 g pro.

Vanilla Panna Cotta

PREP 25 minutes CHILL 4 hours
STAND 5 minutes MAKES 8 servings

1 envelope unflavored gelatin
¼ cup water
½ cup sugar
2 cups whipping cream
1¼ cups sour cream
1½ teaspoons vanilla
1 recipe Cranberry Coulis, Rosemary-Honey Drizzle, or Bittersweet Chocolate Sauce

1. Place eight 4- to 6-ounce ramekins or 6-ounce custard cups in a shallow baking pan; set aside.
2. In a small bowl sprinkle gelatin over the water. Do not stir. Let stand for 5 minutes.
3. Meanwhile, in a medium saucepan combine sugar and ½ cup of the whipping cream. Cook over medium heat until hot but not boiling. Add gelatin mixture, stirring until gelatin is dissolved. Remove from heat. Stir in sour cream until smooth. Stir in the remaining 1½ cups whipping cream and vanilla. Divide mixture among ramekins. Cover and chill for 4 to 24 hours or until set.
4. If desired, unmold panna cotta before serving. Immerse bottom halves of ramekins in hot water for 10 seconds. Using a sharp knife, loosen panna cotta from sides of ramekins. Invert a dessert plate over each ramekin; turn plate and ramekin over together. Remove ramekins. Serve with Cranberry Coulis, Rosemary-Honey Drizzle, or Bittersweet Chocolate Sauce.

Cranberry Coulis In a blender or food processor combine ½ cup canned jellied cranberry sauce and ½ cup thawed, frozen cranberry juice concentrate. Cover and blend or process until smooth.

Bittersweet Chocolate Sauce In a small saucepan combine ½ cup whipping cream and ¼ cup light-color corn syrup. Bring just to boiling over medium heat. Remove from heat. Add 4 ounces chopped bittersweet chocolate (do not stir). Let stand, covered, for 5 minutes. Whisk until smooth. Cool for 15 minutes. Serve warm.

Rosemary-Honey Drizzle In a small saucepan combine ½ cup honey, 2 tablespoons lemon juice, and 2 teaspoons finely snipped fresh rosemary. Bring just to simmering over medium heat, stirring occasionally. Remove from heat; cool slightly. Transfer to a small bowl. Cover and chill for up to 24 hours. Strain honey mixture, discarding rosemary. To speed the preparation, you can cover and freeze the panna cotta for 20 minutes before transferring to the refrigerator. Chill about 1½ hours or until set.
PER SERVING 384 cal., 28 g fat (17 g sat. fat), 98 mg chol., 50 mg sodium, 33 g carb., 0 g fiber, 3 g pro.

SUGAR COOKIES,
PAGE 96

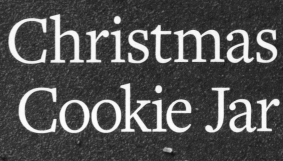

Christmas Cookie Jar

PETITE TREATS The sort of sweet most closely associated with Christmas is the enduring and endearing cookie. Fill your jar here.

MOLASSES
CUTOUTS

CHOCOLATE-CHAI
SHORTBREAD STARS

Molasses Cutouts

PREP **35 minutes** CHILL **3 hours**
BAKE **5 minutes per batch at 375°F**
MAKES **10 servings**

- ½ cup shortening
- ⅔ cup granulated sugar
- 2 teaspoons freshly grated nutmeg or 1½ teaspoons ground nutmeg
- 1 teaspoon baking powder
- ¼ teaspoon salt
- ½ cup mild-flavor molasses
- 1 egg
- 1 tablespoon cider vinegar
- 2½ cups all-purpose flour
  Royal Icing (optional)
  Desired decorations (optional)

1. In a large bowl beat shortening with an electric mixer on medium to high for 30 seconds. Add granulated sugar, nutmeg, baking powder, and salt. Beat until combined, scraping sides of bowl occasionally. Beat in molasses, egg, and vinegar until combined. Beat in as much of the flour as you can with the mixer. Stir in any remaining flour. Divide dough in half. Cover and chill about 3 hours or until dough is easy to handle.
2. Preheat oven to 375°F. Grease a cookie sheet; set aside. On a lightly floured surface roll half of the dough at a time to ⅛ inch thick. Using 2½- to 3-inch cookie cutters, cut into desired shapes. Place 1 inch apart on prepared cookie sheet.
3. Bake for 5 to 6 minutes or until bottoms are light brown. Cool on cookie sheet for 1 minute. Transfer cookies to a wire rack; cool completely. If desired, pipe icing on cookies and decorate.
PER SERVING *86 cal., 3 g fat (1 g sat. fat), 6 mg chol., 27 mg sodium, 14 g carb., 0 g fiber, 1 g pro.*

Royal Icing In a large mixing bowl stir together one 16-ounce package powdered sugar (4¼ cups), 3 tablespoons meringue powder, and ½ teaspoon cream of tartar. Add ½ cup warm water and 1 teaspoon vanilla. Beat with an electric mixer on low until combined; beat on high for 7 to 10 minutes or until icing is very stiff.

Chocolate-Chai Shortbread Stars

PREP **25 minutes**
BAKE **20 minutes at 325°F**
MAKES **20 servings**

- 1¼ cups all-purpose flour
- ⅓ cup sugar
- ¼ cup unsweetened cocoa powder
- ½ teaspoon ground cinnamon
- ½ teaspoon ground ginger
- ½ teaspoon ground cardamom
- ½ teaspoon salt
- ¼ teaspoon ground nutmeg
- ⅛ teaspoon ground cloves
- ½ cup butter
- 2 tablespoons dark chocolate pieces, melted (optional)
- 2 tablespoons white baking pieces, melted (optional)

1. Preheat oven to 325°F. In a medium bowl stir together flour, sugar, cocoa powder, cinnamon, ginger, cardamom, salt, nutmeg, and cloves. Using a pastry blender, cut in butter until mixture resembles fine crumbs and starts to cling. Form the mixture into a ball and knead until smooth.
2. On a lightly floured surface roll dough until ½-inch thickness. Using a 1½- to 2-inch star-shape cookie cutter, cut out dough. Place cutouts 2 inches apart on an ungreased cookie sheet.
3. Bake about 20 minutes or just until cookies are firm in the center. Transfer to a wire rack and let cool. If desired, drizzle cooled cookies with melted dark and/or white chocolate. Let stand until drizzle is set.
PER SERVING *85 cal., 5 g fat (3 g sat. fat), 12 mg chol., 99 mg sodium, 10 g carb., 1 g fiber, 1 g pro.*

RASPBERRY SUGAR
COOKIE SANDWICHES

Raspberry Sugar Cookie Sandwiches

PREP **40 minutes**   CHILL **1 hour**
BAKE **7 minutes per batch at 375°F**
MAKES **20 servings**

- ⅓ cup butter, softened
- ⅓ cup shortening
- ¾ cup granulated sugar
- 1½ teaspoons baking powder
- ¼ teaspoon salt
- ¼ teaspoon ground cinnamon
- ⅛ teaspoon ground cloves
- 1 egg
- 1 tablespoon milk
- ½ teaspoon vanilla
- ½ teaspoon finely shredded lemon peel
- 2 cups all-purpose flour
  Powdered sugar
- ⅓ to ½ cup raspberry, strawberry, or cherry preserves or jam

1. In a large mixing bowl beat butter and shortening with an electric mixer on medium to high for 30 seconds. Add granulated sugar, baking powder, salt, cinnamon, and cloves. Beat until combined, scraping sides of bowl occasionally. Beat in egg, milk, vanilla, and lemon peel until combined. Beat in as much of the flour as you can with the mixer. Using a wooden spoon, stir in any remaining flour. Divide dough in half. Cover and chill dough about 1 hour or until easy to handle.

2. Preheat oven to 375°F. On a lightly floured surface roll half the dough at a time to ⅛- to ¼-inch thickness. Using 2½-inch cookie cutters, cut dough into desired shapes. Place cutouts 1 inch apart on an ungreased cookie sheet. Using ¾-inch cookie cutters, cut desired shapes from centers of half of the cookies. Reroll scraps as necessary.

3. Bake for 7 to 10 minutes or until edges are light brown. Transfer cookies to a wire rack and let cool.

4. Sift powdered sugar onto the cookies with the centers cut out. Spread a scant teaspoon of preserves over the bottoms of the cookies with no cutout centers. Press the bottoms of the sugared cookies against the preserves. Serve within 2 hours.

PER SERVING *154 cal., 7 g fat (3 g sat. fat), 17 mg chol., 89 mg sodium, 22 g carb., 0 g fiber, 2 g pro.*

Sugar Cookies

(photo page 92)

PREP **35 minutes**   CHILL **2 hours**
BAKE **7 minutes at 375°F**
MAKES **10 servings**

- ⅔ cup butter, softened
- ¾ cup sugar

1 teaspoon baking powder
¼ teaspoon salt
1 egg
1 tablespoon milk
1 teaspoon vanilla
2 cups all-purpose flour
   Desired frosting (optional)
   Desired decorations (optional)

1. In a large bowl beat butter with an electric mixer on medium to high for 30 seconds. Add sugar, baking powder, and salt. Beat until combined, scraping bowl occasionally. Beat in egg, milk, and vanilla until combined. Beat in as much of the flour as you can with the mixer. Stir in any remaining flour. Divide dough in half. Cover and chill about 2 hours or until dough is easy to handle.

2. Preheat oven to 375°F. On a lightly floured surface roll half the dough at a time to ¼ inch thick. Using 2½-inch cookie cutters, cut dough into desired shapes. Place cutouts 1 inch apart on an ungreased cookie sheet.

3. Bake for 7 to 10 minutes or until edges are very lightly browned. Transfer to a wire rack; cool completely. If desired, frost and/or decorate cookies.

PER SERVING *74 cal., 4 g fat (2 g sat. fat), 15 mg chol., 49 mg sodium, 10 g carb., 0 g fiber, 1 g pro.*

Cashew Diamonds with Browned Butter Buttercream

PREP **30 minutes** CHILL **1 hour**
BAKE **14 minutes per batch at 350°F**
STAND **5 minutes** MAKES **16 servings**

4 cups all-purpose flour
1 teaspoon baking powder
½ teaspoon salt
½ teaspoon ground cinnamon
2 cups butter, softened
1 cup powdered sugar
½ teaspoon vanilla
1¾ cups roasted salted cashews, finely chopped
1 recipe Browned Butter Buttercream

1. In a medium bowl stir together flour, baking powder, salt, and cinnamon; set aside. In a large mixing bowl beat butter, powdered sugar, and vanilla with an electric mixer on

CASHEW DIAMONDS WITH BROWNED BUTTER BUTTERCREAM

medium until well combined. Add flour mixture; beat on low just until combined. Stir in cashews. Divide dough in half. Form each half into a disk. Cover and chill dough for 1 to 2 hours or until easy to handle.

2. Preheat oven to 350°F. Line two cookie sheets with parchment paper; set aside. On a lightly floured surface roll half the dough at a time to ⅛ inch thickness. Using a 2½-inch scallop-edge, diamond-shape cookie cutter, cut out dough. Place cutouts 1 inch apart on the prepared cookie sheets.

3. Bake for 14 to 16 minutes or until golden. Cool on cookie sheets for 5 minutes. Transfer to a wire rack and let cool.

4. Spread 1 teaspoon of Browned Butter Buttercream on the flat side

(bottom) of 1 cookie. Gently press the flat side of another cookie against the buttercream. Repeat with remaining cookies and buttercream.

Browned Butter Buttercream In a small saucepan over medium heat melt ¼ cup butter. Cook and stir about 5 minutes or until brown and fragrant; let cool. In a large mixing bowl beat ¼ cup softened butter, the cooled browned butter, 2 cups powdered sugar, and 1 teaspoon vanilla with an electric mixer on medium until combined. Beat in 1 to 2 tablespoons buttermilk, 1 teaspoon at a time, until fluffy and spreadable.

PER SERVING *254 cal., 17 g fat (9 g sat. fat), 36 mg chol., 189 mg sodium, 24 g carb., 1 g fiber, 3 g pro.*

Sweet Citrus Krumkaker

PREP 40 minutes STAND 30 minutes
MAKES 10 servings

½ cup butter
3 eggs
½ cup sugar
½ cup all-purpose flour
1 teaspoon vanilla
½ teaspoon finely shredded lemon peel and/or orange peel (optional)
3 ounces vanilla-flavor candy coating
¼ cup crushed lemon drop candies
1 recipe Lemon Cream

1. In a small saucepan melt butter over low heat; set aside to cool slightly. In a medium bowl beat eggs with an electric mixer on medium for 1 minute. Gradually add sugar; beat about 3 minutes or until sugar is almost dissolved, scraping sides of bowl occasionally. Gradually beat in cooled butter until combined. Stir in flour, vanilla, and, if desired, shredded lemon peel just until mixture is combined and smooth.
2. Heat a nonelectric krumkake iron on the range top over medium-low heat. Lightly grease the krumkake grid. If using a 6-inch iron, spoon

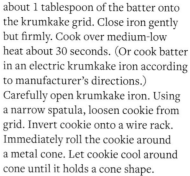

SWEET CITRUS KRUMKAKER

about 1 tablespoon of the batter onto the krumkake grid. Close iron gently but firmly. Cook over medium-low heat about 30 seconds. (Or cook batter in an electric krumkake iron according to manufacturer's directions.) Carefully open krumkake iron. Using a narrow spatula, loosen cookie from grid. Invert cookie onto a wire rack. Immediately roll the cookie around a metal cone. Let cookie cool around cone until it holds a cone shape.
3. Repeat, heating the krumkake iron and cooking the remaining batter 1 tablespoon at a time. Completely cool the rolled cookie cones on wire racks.
4. To decorate cookies, in a small microwave-safe bowl heat the candy coating, uncovered, on high for 30 to 60 seconds or until melted and smooth, stirring twice. Place crushed lemon drops in a small shallow bowl.
5. Carefully dip the rim of a cookie into melted candy coating, letting excess drip back into bowl. Immediately dip rim into crushed lemon drops to coat. Place krumkake on a cookie sheet lined with waxed paper. Repeat with remaining cookies, candy coating, and crushed lemon drops. Let stand about 30 minutes or until set.
6. To fill krumkaker, spoon Lemon Cream into a decorating bag fitted with a large star tip. Pipe cream into the cones. Serve immediately.
Lemon Cream In a medium bowl combine two 8-ounce packages softened cream cheese and one 10-ounce jar lemon curd. Beat with an electric mixer on medium until mixture is combined and smooth.
PER SERVING 159 cal., 10 g fat (6 g sat. fat), 53 mg chol., 85 mg sodium, 16 g carb., 1 g fiber, 2 g pro.

Chocolate-Glazed Madeleines

PREP 25 minutes
BAKE 10 minutes at 375°F
CHILL 30 minutes
MAKES 24 servings

½ cup sugar
2 egg yolks
½ cup butter, melted and cooled
½ teaspoon finely shredded orange peel
1 tablespoon orange-flavor liqueur or orange juice
1 teaspoon vanilla
½ cup all-purpose flour
½ teaspoon baking powder
⅛ teaspoon baking soda
⅛ teaspoon salt
2 egg whites, lightly beaten
1 recipe Chocolate Glaze
Finely chopped pistachios (optional)

1. Grease and flour twenty-four 3-inch madeleine molds. Set molds aside. Preheat oven to 375°F.
2. In a medium bowl beat sugar and egg yolks with electric mixer on medium to high about 30 seconds or until combined. Add the melted butter, orange peel, orange liqueur, and vanilla. Beat on low until combined.
3. In a small bowl combine the flour, baking powder, baking soda, and salt. Sprinkle about one-fourth of the flour mixture over the egg-yolk mixture; stir in gently. Repeat, sprinkling and stirring in one-fourth of the flour mixture at a time. Gently stir in the egg whites.
4. Spoon the batter into the molds, filling each mold about one-half full.
5. Bake in the preheated oven for 10 to 12 minutes or until edges are golden brown and tops spring back when lightly touched. Cool in molds for 1 minute. Using the point of a knife, loosen each madeleine from the mold; invert mold onto a wire rack. Remove mold. Transfer madeleines to a wire rack; cool completely.
6. Dip half of each cookie in warm Chocolate Glaze, letting excess drip off. Place on a waxed paper-lined pan. If desired, sprinkle pistachios onto Chocolate Glaze. Chill madeleines about 30 minutes or until Chocolate Glaze is set.
Chocolate Glaze In a medium saucepan heat ½ cup whipping cream, ½ teaspoon vanilla, and, if desired, 1 tablespoon orange-flavor liqueur over medium-high heat until just boiling. Remove from heat. Add 6 ounces bittersweet or semisweet chocolate, chopped. Do not stir. Let stand for 5 minutes; stir until smooth.
PER SERVING 126 cal., 9 g fat (6 g sat. fat), 52 mg chol., 62 mg sodium, 10 g carb., 1 g fiber, 2 g pro.

CHOCOLATE-GLAZED
MADELEINES

VANILLA-STAR ANISE
CRESCENTS

Vanilla-Star Anise Crescents

PREP 30 minutes CHILL 1 hour
BAKE 8 minutes per batch at 350°F
COOL 5 minutes MAKES 48 servings

1 vanilla bean, split lengthwise
2 cups powdered sugar
⅛ teaspoon Chinese five-spice powder
1½ cups butter, softened
½ cup granulated sugar
2 cups slivered almonds, finely ground
½ teaspoon salt
3 cups all-purpose flour

1. Using the tip of a small sharp knife, scrape out the seeds from the vanilla bean. In a food processor process the powdered sugar, vanilla seeds, and five-spice powder until vanilla seeds are well incorporated. Set aside.
2. In a large bowl beat butter with an electric mixer on medium to high for 30 seconds. Add the granulated sugar, almonds, and salt. Beat until combined, scraping sides of bowl occasionally. Beat in as much of the flour as you can with the mixer. Stir in any remaining flour. Cover and chill dough about 1 hour or until easy to handle.
3. Preheat oven to 350°F. Lightly grease cookie sheets. Shape dough into 1-inch balls, then mold into a crescent shape. Place crescents 2 inches apart on the prepared cookie sheets.
4. Bake for 8 to 10 minutes or until set and edges are golden. Cool on cookie sheets for 5 minutes. While warm, roll cookies in powdered sugar mixture. Transfer to a wire rack and let cool. Roll cooled cookies in the powdered sugar mixture again.

PER SERVING 133 cal., 8 g fat (4 g sat. fat), 15 mg chol., 75 mg sodium, 14 g carb., 1 g fiber, 2 g pro.

Chocolate-Peppermint Waffle Cookies

PREP 30 minutes
COOK 1 minute per batch
MAKES 36 servings

1 cup butter
4 ounces unsweetened chocolate, chopped

CHOCOLATE-PEPPERMINT WAFFLE COOKIES

1½ cups granulated sugar
4 eggs
2 teaspoons vanilla
½ teaspoon salt
½ teaspoon instant coffee crystals
½ cup unsweetened cocoa powder
1½ cups all-purpose flour
2 tablespoons butter
¼ cup powdered sugar
2 tablespoons unsweetened cocoa powder
1 to 2 tablespoons milk
¼ teaspoon peppermint extract
Crushed peppermint candies

1. In a saucepan heat and stir the 1 cup butter and unsweetened chocolate over low heat until melted and smooth. Remove from heat and let cool slightly.
2. In a large mixing bowl beat the granulated sugar, eggs, vanilla, salt, and coffee crystals with an electric mixer on medium to high about 4 minutes or until thick and pale. Beat in the melted chocolate mixture. Beat in the ½ cup of cocoa powder and as much of the flour as

you can with the mixer. Stir in any remaining flour.
3. Heat an electric waffle iron according to manufacturer's directions. Lightly grease the grids. Spoon 2 tablespoons batter into the center of each waffle section to make 1½- to 2-inch cookies. Close the iron and cook for 1 to 1½ minutes or until set. Using a fork, loosen the cookies from the grid. Transfer to a wire rack and let cool. Repeat with remaining batter, lightly greasing grids after each batch.
4. In a saucepan melt the 2 tablespoons butter over low heat. Remove from heat. Stir in the powdered sugar and the 2 tablespoons cocoa powder until smooth. Stir in the milk and peppermint extract to make a thin glaze.
5. Dip one side of each cookie in the glaze to coat the top, allowing excess glaze to drip off. Transfer to a parchment-lined baking sheet; sprinkle with crushed peppermint candies. Let stand until set.

PER SERVING 145 cal., 8 g fat (5 g sat. fat), 36 mg chol., 93 mg sodium, 18 g carb., 1 g fiber, 2 g pro.

Chocolate-Malted Milk Biscotti

PREP 30 minutes
BAKE 41 minutes at 325°F
COOL 1 hour MAKES 30 servings

1¾ cups all-purpose flour
¾ cup unsweetened cocoa powder
¼ cup malted milk powder
1 teaspoon baking soda
½ teaspoon salt
3 eggs
¼ cup butter, melted
1 cup sugar
1 teaspoon vanilla
1 cup coarsely chopped malted
    milk balls
½ cup milk chocolate pieces

1. Preheat oven to 325°F. Line large cookie sheet with parchment paper; set aside.
2. In a large bowl stir together flour, cocoa powder, malted milk powder, baking soda, and salt. Make a well in the center of the flour mixture; set aside. In a medium mixing bowl whisk together eggs, melted butter, sugar, and vanilla. Add egg mixture to the flour mixture; stir until the dough starts to form a ball. Stir in malted milk balls and chocolate pieces (dough will be crumbly). Knead the dough until it comes together.
3. Turn the dough out onto a lightly floured surface. Divide dough in half. Shape each half into a 10-inch-long roll. Place rolls about 3 inches apart on the prepared cookie sheet; flatten slightly until about 2 inches wide.
4. Bake for 25 minutes. Cool on cookie sheet on a wire rack for at least 1 hour.
5. Transfer rolls to a cutting board. Using a serrated knife, cut each roll diagonally into ½-inch slices. Place slices, cut sides down, on cookie sheet. Bake for 8 minutes. Turn slices over and bake for 8 minutes more. Transfer to a wire rack and let cool. (Cookies will crisp as they cool.)
PER SERVING *100 cal., 3 g fat (2 g sat. fat), 20 mg chol., 99 mg sodium, 16 g carb., 1 g fiber, 2 g pro.*

Salted Caramel-Ginger Macarons

PREP 45 minutes STAND 30 minutes
BAKE 9 minutes per batch at 325°F
MAKES 30 servings

1½ cups finely ground almonds
1¼ cups powdered sugar
1½ teaspoons ground ginger
3 egg whites
½ teaspoon vanilla
    Dash salt
¼ cup granulated sugar
6 drops yellow food coloring
½ of a 14-ounce package vanilla
    caramels, unwrapped
2 tablespoons whipping cream
    Coarse sea salt

1. Line three large cookie sheets with parchment paper; set aside. In a medium bowl stir together almonds, powdered sugar, and ginger; set aside.
2. In a large bowl combine egg whites, vanilla, and salt. Beat with an electric mixer on medium until frothy. Gradually add granulated sugar, about 1 tablespoon at a time, beating on high just until soft peaks form (tips curl). Stir in nut mixture and food coloring.
3. Spoon mixture into a large decorating bag fitted with a large (about ½-inch) round tip.* Pipe 1½-inch circles 1 inch apart onto the prepared cookie sheets. Let stand for 30 minutes before baking.
4. Meanwhile, preheat oven to 325°F. Bake for 9 to 10 minutes or until set. Cool on cookie sheets on wire racks. Carefully peel cookies off parchment paper.
5. In a small saucepan combine caramels and cream; heat and stir over low heat until melted and smooth. Spread caramel mixture on bottoms of half of the cookies; immediately after spreading, sprinkle each with a little coarse sea salt. Top with the remaining cookies, bottom sides down.
*If you don't have a decorating bag, spoon mixture into a large resealable plastic bag and snip a ½-inch hole in one corner of the bag.
PER SERVING *85 cal., 3 g fat (1 g sat. fat), 1 mg chol., 40 mg sodium, 12 g carb., 1 g fiber, 2 g pro.*

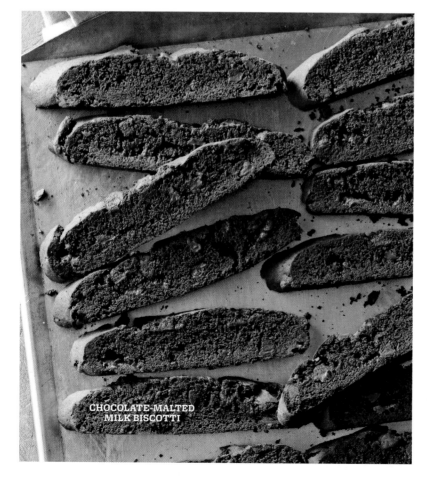

CHOCOLATE-MALTED
MILK BISCOTTI

SALTED CARAMEL-
GINGER MACARONS

May all the
Christmas Joys
be Yours

MINT MERINGUE
KISSES

Mint Meringue Kisses

PREP **35 minutes**
BAKE **1 hour at 225°F**
STAND **1 hour**   MAKES **30 servings**

4   egg whites
½   teaspoon cream of tartar
½   teaspoon salt
1⅓ cups sugar
¼   teaspoon mint extract
7   to 8 drops green food coloring
2   ounces semisweet chocolate,
    chopped
½   teaspoon vegetable oil

1. Allow egg whites to stand at room temperature for 30 minutes. Preheat oven to 225°F. Line a large cookie sheet with parchment paper; set aside. In a large mixing bowl add cream of tartar and salt to egg whites. Beat with an electric mixer on high until soft peaks form (tips curl). Gradually add sugar, 1 tablespoon at a time, beating on high until glossy and stiff peaks form (tips stand straight). Beat in mint extract and green food coloring.
2. Transfer meringue to a pastry bag fitted with a ½- to ¾-inch open star tip. Pipe stars 1 inch apart onto the prepared cookie sheet. Bake about 60 minutes or until meringues appear dry and are firm when lightly touched. Turn off oven. Let meringues stand in the closed oven about 60 minutes or until cool and crisp.
3. In a small saucepan heat and stir 2 ounces chocolate and the vegetable oil over low heat until melted and smooth. Spread about ½ teaspoon each melted chocolate on the flat sides (bottoms) of half the meringues. Press the flat sides of the remaining cookies against the filling. Let stand until set.
PER SERVING *47 cal., 1 g fat, (0 g sat. fat), 0 mg chol., 46 mg sodium, 10 g carb., 0 g fiber, 1 g pro.*

Pumpkin Whoopie Pies with Maple-Browned Butter Filling

PREP **45 minutes**
BAKE **12 minutes per batch at 350°F**
CHILL **30 minutes**   MAKES **36 servings**

3   cups all-purpose flour
2   teaspoons ground cinnamon

PUMPKIN WHOOPIE PIES WITH MAPLE-BROWNED BUTTER FILLING

1   teaspoon baking powder
1   teaspoon baking soda
1   teaspoon salt
1   teaspoon ground ginger
¼   teaspoon ground cloves
¼   teaspoon ground anise
    (optional)
2   cups packed dark brown sugar
¾   cup vegetable oil
¼   cup butter, melted and cooled
2   eggs
2¾ cups canned pumpkin
1½ teaspoons vanilla
1   recipe Maple-Browned Butter
    Filling

1. Preheat oven to 350°F. Line a cookie sheet with parchment paper. In a medium bowl stir together flour, cinnamon, baking powder, baking soda, salt, ginger, cloves, and, if desired, anise. Set aside.
2. In a large mixing bowl beat brown sugar, oil, and melted butter with an electric mixer on medium until combined. Add eggs, pumpkin, and vanilla; beat for 1 minute. Add flour mixture, half at a time, beating well after each addition (batter will resemble a thick cake batter).
3. Drop batter by rounded tablespoons 1½ inches apart onto the prepared cookie sheet. Bake for 12 to 14 minutes

or until tops spring back when lightly touched. Cool on cookie sheet for 5 minutes. Transfer to a wire rack; cool completely.
4. Spread about 2 teaspoons of the Maple-Browned Butter Filling on bottoms of half of the cookies. Top with the remaining cookies, bottom sides together; press down gently to spread filling. Chill, uncovered, for 30 minutes before serving.
Maple-Browned Butter Filling In a small saucepan heat 5 tablespoons butter over medium-low heat until melted. Continue heating until butter turns a light golden brown. Cool for 15 minutes. In a medium mixing bowl beat browned butter and 4 ounces softened cream cheese with an electric mixer on medium about 2 minutes or until fluffy. Add 1 tablespoon maple syrup, ¼ teaspoon ground cinnamon, ¼ teaspoon ground nutmeg, ⅛ teaspoon salt, and dash ground cloves; beat on low until combined. Gradually beat in 3 to 3½ cups powdered sugar to reach spreading consistency.
PER SERVING *510 cal., 21 g fat (7 g sat. fat), 51 mg chol., 397 mg sodium, 77 g carb., 2 g fiber, 5 g pro.*

CHERRY PIE BITES

Cherry Pie Bites

PREP **30 minutes**
BAKE **25 minutes at 325°F**
COOL **5 minutes** MAKES **24 servings**

- ½ cup butter, softened
- 1 3-ounce package cream cheese, softened
- 1 cup all-purpose flour
- 2 tablespoons all-purpose flour
- 2 tablespoons chopped toasted walnuts or pecans
- 2 tablespoons packed brown sugar
- ⅛ teaspoon ground nutmeg
- 1½ tablespoons butter
- 2 cups fresh or frozen unsweetened pitted tart red cherries, thawed
- ⅓ cup granulated sugar
- 2 teaspoons cornstarch

1. Preheat oven to 325°F. In a medium mixing bowl beat the ½ cup butter and the cream cheese with an electric mixer on medium to high until combined. Stir in the 1 cup flour. Shape dough into 24 balls. Press the balls evenly into the bottoms and up the sides of 24 ungreased 1¾-inch muffin cups.
2. For streusel, in a small bowl stir together the 2 tablespoons flour, the walnuts, brown sugar, and nutmeg.

Using a pastry blender, cut in the 1½ tablespoons butter until mixture is crumbly. Set aside.
3. For filling, in a small saucepan combine the cherries, granulated sugar, and cornstarch. Cook over medium heat until cherries release juices, stirring occasionally. Continue to cook, stirring constantly, over medium heat until thick and bubbly. Spoon about 1 heaping teaspoon of the filling into each pastry-lined cup. Sprinkle filled cups evenly with streusel.
4. Bake for 25 to 30 minutes or until edges are golden brown. Cool bites in pan on a wire rack for 5 minutes. Carefully transfer to a wire rack and let cool.

PER SERVING *100 cal., 6 g fat (4 g sat. fat), 16 mg chol., 52 mg sodium, 10 g carb., 0 g fiber, 1 g pro.*

Chocolate Walnut Tassies

PREP **40 minutes**
BAKE **16 minutes at 325°F**
COOL **10 minutes** MAKES **16 servings**

- 2 ounces sweet baking chocolate, chopped
- 1 3-ounce package cream cheese, softened
- ⅓ cup butter, softened
- 1 cup all-purpose flour
- 1 cup semisweet chocolate pieces
- ⅓ cup light-color corn syrup
- ¼ cup granulated sugar
- 1 tablespoon butter
- 1 tablespoon unsweetened cocoa powder
- 1 teaspoon instant coffee crystals or ½ teaspoon instant espresso coffee powder
- ¼ teaspoon salt
- 1 egg, lightly beaten
- 1 egg yolk
- 1 tablespoon dark rum (optional)
- 30 walnut halves
  Cocoa powder or powdered sugar (optional)

1. For pastry, in a small saucepan heat and stir the sweet baking chocolate over low heat until melted and smooth. Cool slightly (10 to 15 minutes). In a medium mixing bowl beat the melted chocolate, cream cheese, and the ⅓ cup butter with an electric mixer on medium until combined. Beat in the flour until combined. If necessary, cover and chill dough about 1 hour or until easy to handle.
2. Preheat oven to 325°F. Shape dough into 30 balls. Press each ball into the bottoms and up the sides of thirty 1¾-inch muffin cups. Set aside.
3. For filling, in a medium microwave-safe bowl combine semisweet chocolate pieces, corn syrup, granulated sugar, the 1 tablespoon butter, the cocoa powder, coffee crystals, and salt. Microwave on high for 1 to 1½ minutes or until chocolate melts and mixture is smooth, stirring every 30 seconds. Stir in the egg, egg yolk, and, if desired, rum. Spoon filling evenly into pastry-lined cups and top each with a walnut half.
4. Bake for 16 to 20 minutes or until filling is just set. Cool tassies in pan on a wire rack for 10 minutes. Carefully transfer to a wire rack and let cool. If desired, dust with cocoa powder just before serving.

PER SERVING *122 cal., 8 g fat (4 g sat. fat), 22 mg chol., 56 mg sodium, 13 g carb., 1 g fiber, 2 g pro.*

CHOCOLATE WALNUT
TASSIES

ALMOND-APRICOT
BLONDIES

Almond-Apricot Blondies

PREP 30 minutes
BAKE 35 minutes at 350°F
MAKES 32 servings

- 1 cup dried apricots, coarsely snipped
- ¼ cup amaretto or apricot nectar
- 2 cups packed brown sugar
- ⅔ cup butter
- 2 eggs
- 2 teaspoons vanilla
- 2 cups all-purpose flour
- 1 teaspoon baking powder
- ¼ teaspoon baking soda
- ¼ teaspoon salt
- 2 cups sliced almonds, toasted (see tip, page 25)
- 1 cup apricot preserves

1. In a small saucepan combine dried apricots and amaretto. Bring just to boiling; cool. Preheat oven to 350°F. Line a 13×9×2-inch baking pan with foil, extending the foil over edges of pan. Lightly grease foil; set pan aside.
2. In a medium saucepan cook and stir brown sugar and butter over medium heat until melted and smooth; cool slightly. Add eggs, one at a time, beating with a wooden spoon after each addition just until combined. Stir in vanilla. Stir in flour, baking powder, baking soda, and salt until combined. Stir in undrained apricots. Fold in 1½ cups of the almonds. Spread batter evenly in the prepared baking pan.
3. Bake about 35 minutes or until a wooden toothpick inserted near the center comes out clean. Cool slightly in pan on a wire rack.
4. Meanwhile, in a small saucepan bring apricot preserves to boiling over medium-high heat. Reduce heat to medium-low; simmer, uncovered, about 10 minutes or until slightly thickened. Cool for 5 minutes.
5. Gently spread preserves over warm uncut bars. Sprinkle with remaining ½ cup almonds. Using the edges of the foil, lift uncut bars out of pan. Cut into bars.
PER SERVING 198 cal., 7 g fat (3 g sat. fat), 22 mg chol., 89 mg sodium, 31 g carb., 1 g fiber, 3 g pro.

BLONDIE STIX

Blondie Stix

PREP 1 hour
BAKE 30 minutes at 350°F
FREEZE 30 minutes   STAND 1 hour
MAKES 32 servings

- 2 cups all-purpose flour
- 2½ teaspoons baking powder
- ½ teaspoon salt
- 2 cups packed brown sugar
- ¾ cup butter, softened
- 1 teaspoon vanilla
- 3 eggs
- 1 cup tiny marshmallows
- 1 cup chopped unsalted cashews or toffee pieces
- 1 11.5- to 12-ounce package bittersweet chocolate pieces or white baking pieces

1. Preheat oven to 350°F. Line a 13×9×2-inch baking pan with foil, extending foil over short ends of pan. Grease foil; set pan aside.
2. In a small bowl combine flour, baking powder, and salt; set aside. In a large bowl combine brown sugar, butter, and vanilla. Beat with an electric mixer on medium-high until combined. Beat in eggs, one at a time, beating well after each addition.

Gradually beat in flour mixture. Stir in marshmallows. Spread dough in prepared pan.
3. Bake about 30 minutes or until top is golden and edges are firm. Cool on a wire rack. Using the edges of the foil, lift uncut brownies out of pan. Invert onto a cutting board; remove foil. Trim edges of uncut brownies to make a 12×8-inch rectangle. Cut rectangle into thirty-two 3×1-inch sticks. Cover and freeze about 30 minutes or until firm.
4. Insert a 6- to 8-inch wooden skewer into an end of each brownie stick and place on a waxed paper-lined baking sheet. Place cashews in a small shallow bowl. In a small saucepan cook and stir chocolate pieces over low heat until melted.
5. Dip half of each brownie stick into melted chocolate, allowing excess chocolate to drip back into saucepan. Immediately sprinkle with cashews. Place on prepared baking sheet. Let stand about 1 hour or until chocolate is set.
PER SERVING 211 cal., 11 g fat (6 g sat. fat), 32 mg chol., 109 mg sodium, 28 g carb., 1 g fiber, 3 g pro.

BLOOD ORANGE BARS

Blood Orange Bars

PREP **30 minutes**
BAKE **35 minutes at 350°F**
MAKES **16 servings**

- 1 cup all-purpose flour
- 3 tablespoons powdered sugar
- ¼ teaspoon salt
- ⅓ cup butter
- 1 cup granulated sugar
- 2 eggs
- 2 teaspoons finely shredded blood orange peel or orange peel
- ⅔ cup fresh blood orange juice or orange juice
- 2 drops red food coloring (optional)
- 2 tablespoons all-purpose flour
- ¼ teaspoon salt
  Powdered sugar

1. Preheat oven to 350°F. Line an 8×8×2-inch baking pan with foil, extending the foil over the edges of the pan. Grease foil; set aside.
2. For crust, in a large bowl stir together the 1 cup flour, the 3 tablespoons powdered sugar, and the ¼ teaspoon salt. Using a pastry blender, cut in butter until mixture resembles coarse crumbs. Press mixture evenly and firmly into the bottom of the prepared pan. Bake about 15 minutes or until light golden around the edges.
3. In a medium bowl whisk together the granulated sugar, eggs, orange peel, orange juice, and food coloring (if using) until smooth. Stir in the 2 tablespoons flour and the ¼ teaspoon salt. Pour orange mixture over the hot crust.
4. Bake for 20 to 25 minutes or until set. Cool completely in pan on a wire rack. Use foil to lift uncut bars out of pan. Place on a cutting board. Cut into bars. Dust bars with powdered sugar.*
*Place a snowflake- or other-shape stencil on each bar before dusting with the powdered sugar.
PER SERVING *138 cal., 5 g fat (3 g sat. fat), 33 mg chol., 116 mg sodium, 23 g carb., 0 g fiber, 2 g pro.*

Marbled Chocolate-Pumpkin Brownies

PREP **30 minutes**
BAKE **1 hour at 325°F**
MAKES **36 servings**

- 1 3-ounce package cream cheese, softened
- 1 tablespoon butter, softened
- ½ cup sugar
- 1 egg
- 1 cup canned pumpkin
- 1 teaspoon vanilla
- ½ teaspoon ground cinnamon
- ¼ teaspoon ground ginger
- 1 tablespoon all-purpose flour
- 1¼ cups all-purpose flour
- ¾ teaspoon baking powder
- ½ teaspoon salt
- 6 ounces unsweetened chocolate, chopped
- ¾ cup butter, cut up
- 2¼ cups sugar
- 4 eggs
- ¼ cup milk
- 2 teaspoons vanilla
- ¾ cup coarsely chopped toasted walnuts (see tip, page 25) (optional)

1. Preheat oven to 325°F. Line a 13×9×2-inch baking pan with foil, extending the foil over edges of pan. Grease foil; set pan aside.
2. In a medium mixing bowl beat cream cheese and 1 tablespoon butter with an electric mixer on medium to high for 30 seconds. Add ½ cup sugar. Beat until combined, scraping sides of bowl occasionally. Beat in 1 egg, pumpkin, 1 teaspoon vanilla, cinnamon, and ginger until combined. Stir in 1 tablespoon flour; set aside.
3. In a small bowl stir together 1¼ cups flour, baking powder, and salt; set aside. In a large saucepan cook and stir chocolate and ¾ cup butter over low heat until melted. Remove from heat. Gradually add 2¼ cups sugar, beating on low just until combined. Add 4 eggs, one at a time, beating well after each addition. Beat in milk and 2 teaspoons vanilla. Gradually beat in flour mixture just until combined.
4. Spread chocolate batter in the prepared baking pan. Spoon cream cheese mixture into small mounds on top of chocolate batter. Using a narrow metal spatula or a table knife, swirl gently to marble. If desired, sprinkle with walnuts.
5. Bake about 1 hour or just until center is set when pan is gently shaken. Cool in pan on a wire rack. Using the edges of the foil, lift uncut brownies out of pan. Cut into bars.
PER SERVING *159 cal., 8 g fat (5 g sat. fat), 43 mg chol., 92 mg sodium, 21 g carb., 1 g fiber, 2 g pro.*

CHOCOLATE-
RASPBERRY
CHEESECAKE BARS

Chocolate-Raspberry Cheesecake Bars

PREP **30 minutes**
BAKE **25 minutes at 350°F**
CHILL **1 hour**   MAKES **16 servings**

  1 cup crushed chocolate wafer cookies (about 20 cookies)
  3 tablespoons butter, melted
  ½ of an 8-ounce package cream cheese, softened
  ⅓ cup sour cream
  ¼ cup granulated sugar
  1 egg
  1 tablespoon raspberry liqueur (optional)
  1 teaspoon cornstarch
  ½ teaspoon finely shredded lemon peel
  1 cup fresh raspberries
    Seedless raspberry jam or currant jelly, melted (optional)

1. Preheat oven to 350°F. Line an 8×8×2-inch baking pan with foil, extending the foil over the edges of the pan. Lightly grease the foil. In a small bowl stir together wafer crumbs and melted butter. Pat crumb mixture firmly into the bottom of the prepared pan; set aside.
2. In a medium mixing bowl beat cream cheese with an electric mixer on medium to high until smooth. Add sour cream and granulated sugar. Beat until combined, scraping sides of bowl occasionally. Beat in the egg just until combined. Add the raspberry liqueur (if using), the cornstarch, and lemon peel. Beat on low just until combined. Pour the cream cheese mixture over the crust in pan, spreading evenly. Arrange the raspberries on the cream cheese mixture.
3. Bake for 25 to 30 minutes or until center is set. Cool in pan on a wire rack. Cover and chill for at least 1 hour or overnight. If desired, drizzle melted seedless raspberry jam on raspberries before serving.
PER SERVING *106 cal., 7 g fat (4 g sat. fat), 27 mg chol., 101 mg sodium, 10 g carb., 1 g fiber, 2 g pro.*

Outrageous Oatmeal Cookies

PREP **25 minutes**
BAKE **8 minutes per batch at 350°F**
COOL **2 minutes**   MAKES **60 servings**

2½ cups rolled oats
  ½ cup butter, softened
  ½ cup shortening
  1 cup packed brown sugar
  ½ cup granulated sugar
  1 teaspoon baking powder
  1 teaspoon baking soda
  ½ teaspoon salt
  2 eggs
  ⅓ cup molasses
1½ teaspoons vanilla
2¼ cups all-purpose flour
  1 cup snipped dried figs
  1 cup chopped toasted pecans
  ½ cup dried cranberries or cherries
  ⅓ cup dry-roasted sunflower kernels

1. Preheat oven to 350°F. Line cookie sheets with parchment paper; set aside. In a food processor or a blender process oats to a fine powder; set aside.
2. In a large mixing bowl beat butter and shortening with an electric mixer on medium to high for 30 seconds. Add the brown sugar, granulated sugar, baking powder, baking soda, and salt. Beat until combined, scraping sides of bowl occasionally. Beat in the eggs, molasses, and vanilla until combined. Beat in the flour and as much of the ground oats as you can with the mixer. Stir in any remaining oats, the figs, pecans, cranberries, and sunflower kernels.
3. Drop dough by rounded teaspoons 2 inches apart onto the prepared cookie sheets. Bake for 8 to 10 minutes or until golden brown. Cool on cookie sheets for 2 minutes. Transfer to a wire rack and let cool.
PER SERVING *111 cal., 5 g fat (2 g sat. fat), 10 mg chol., 67 mg sodium, 15 g carb., 1 g fiber, 2 g pro.*

Sweet Confections

DANDY CANDY Turn your kitchen into a candy shop this season. Prettily presented, these simple truffles, fudges, barks, and toffees make great gifts or impressive additions to your holiday dessert table.

NO-BAKE PEANUT BUTTER
BALLS, PAGE 117

SALTED NUT TRUFFLES

Salted Nut Truffles

PREP **45 minutes** STAND **30 minutes**
MAKES **56 servings**

- 1 7-ounce jar marshmallow creme
- 1 cup creamy peanut butter
- 1 cup powdered sugar
- ¾ cup lightly salted cocktail peanuts, finely chopped
- 2 tablespoons light-color corn syrup
- 2 cups white baking pieces or milk chocolate pieces
- 1 tablespoon shortening
  Finely chopped cocktail peanuts or chocolate-flavor sprinkles (jimmies) (optional)

1. Line a baking sheet or tray with waxed paper. In a large microwave-safe bowl combine marshmallow creme and peanut butter. Heat, uncovered, on high for 30 seconds or until mixture is slightly softened, stirring once. Stir in powdered sugar, the ¾ cup finely chopped peanuts, and corn syrup until mixture is well combined.

2. Shape the peanut butter mixture into 1-inch balls. Place balls on the prepared baking sheet.

3. In a small microwave-safe bowl heat white baking pieces and shortening, uncovered, on medium about 2 minutes or until chocolate melts, stirring twice.

4. Using a fork, dip balls into melted mixture, allowing excess mixture to drip back into bowl. Return balls to prepared baking sheet. If desired sprinkle truffles with additional finely chopped peanuts or chocolate sprinkles. Let stand about 30 minutes or until set. Or, if necessary, chill to set.

PER SERVING *107 cal., 6 g fat (3 g sat. fat), 0 g chol., 42 mg sodium, 12 g carb., 0 g fiber, 2 g pro.*

No-Bake Peanut Butter Balls

PREP **30 minutes**
CHILL **50 minutes** COOL **5 minutes**
MAKES **50 servings**

- 1 cup crunchy peanut butter
- ¼ cup butter, softened
- 1 cup powdered sugar

NO-BAKE PEANUT BUTTER BALLS

- 2 tablespoons unsweetened cocoa powder
- 2 cups crispy rice cereal
- 2 cups dry-roasted peanuts, chopped
- 8 ounces semisweet chocolate, chopped
- 8 ounces chocolate-flavor candy coating
- 1 tablespoon shortening

1. Line a large baking sheet with parchment paper; set aside. In a large mixing bowl beat peanut butter and butter with an electric mixer on medium to high for 30 seconds. Beat in powdered sugar and unsweetened cocoa powder on low until combined. Using a wooden spoon, stir in rice cereal and 1 cup of the chopped peanuts. Cover and chill for 1 hour or until easy to handle.

2. With buttered hands, shape mixture into 1-inch balls. Place balls on prepared baking sheet; chill for 30 minutes.

3. In a small heavy saucepan heat and stir semisweet chocolate, chocolate candy coating, and shortening over low heat until melted and smooth. Cool about 5 minutes or until slightly thickened.

4. Line a large baking sheet with waxed paper. Using a fork, dip chilled balls, one at a time, into chocolate mixture, allowing excess to drip off. Place on the prepared baking sheet. Sprinkle each ball immediately with about ½ teaspoon of the remaining chopped peanuts. Chill balls about 20 minutes or until firm.

PER SERVING *136 cal., 10 g fat (4 g sat. fat), 2 mg chol., 39 mg sodium, 12 g carb., 1 g fiber, 3 g pro.*

DOUBLE-DECKER LAYERED FUDGE

Double-Decker Layered Fudge

PREP 30 minutes COOK 10 minutes
COOL 15 minutes CHILL 2 hours
MAKES 64 servings

- 2 cups sugar
- 1 cup evaporated milk
- ¼ teaspoon salt
- 1 12-ounce package white baking pieces
- 1 7-ounce jar marshmallow creme
- 2½ teaspoons vanilla
- 4 ounces dark chocolate, chopped (¾ cup)

1. Line an 8×8×2-inch baking pan with foil, extending the foil over edges of pan. Butter foil; set pan aside.
2. Butter the sides of a 3-quart heavy saucepan. In the saucepan combine sugar, evaporated milk, and salt. Cook and stir over medium-high heat until mixture boils. Reduce heat to medium; continue cooking for 10 minutes, stirring occasionally.
3. Remove saucepan from heat. Add white baking pieces and marshmallow creme. Beat mixture vigorously with a clean wooden spoon for 1 to 2 minutes or until mixture starts to thicken. Pour half of the mixture (about 2 cups) into a bowl. For the white chocolate layer, stir 2 teaspoons of the vanilla into mixture in bowl; set aside.
4. For the dark chocolate layer, add the 4 ounces chopped dark chocolate and the remaining ½ teaspoon vanilla into mixture in saucepan; stir until chocolate melts and mixture is smooth. Remove ⅓ cup of the dark chocolate mixture; set aside. Immediately spread remaining dark chocolate mixture evenly in the prepared pan.
5. Gently spoon the white chocolate mixture in bowl over the dark chocolate mixture; spread fudge evenly to edges of pan. Marble in the reserved dark chocolate mixture. Cool for 15 minutes.
6. Cover; chill for 2 to 3 hours or until firm. When fudge is firm, using the edges of the foil, lift fudge out of pan. Cut fudge into squares.
PER SERVING *80 cal., 3 g fat (2 g sat. fat), 2 mg chol., 22 mg sodium, 13 g carb., 0 g fiber, 1 g pro.*

Cranberry-Cashew Clusters

PREP 25 minutes STAND 30 minutes
MAKES 72 servings

- 1 cup puffed rice cereal
- 1 cup lightly salted cashews, coarsely chopped
- ½ cup dried cranberries, chopped
- 10 ounces vanilla-flavor candy coating, chopped
  Dash freshly grated nutmeg or ground nutmeg
  Dash ground cinnamon
- 1 ounce semisweet chocolate pieces
- 1 teaspoon shortening
  Finely chopped cashews

1. Line a large baking sheet with foil; set aside. Place puffed rice cereal in a resealable plastic bag; seal bag. Using a rolling pin, roll over bag to crush cereal lightly. In a large bowl combine crushed cereal, the 1 cup cashews, and the cranberries; set aside.
2. In a medium microwave-safe bowl heat candy coating, nutmeg, and cinnamon, uncovered, on high for 1 to 1½ minutes or until candy coating melts, stirring every 30 seconds. Pour melted candy coating mixture over cereal mixture; stir until thoroughly combined.
3. Quickly drop spoonfuls of the mixture onto the prepared baking sheet. Let clusters stand about 30 minutes or until firm. In a small saucepan heat chocolate pieces and shortening over low heat until melted and smooth. Drizzle clusters with melted chocolate mixture. Sprinkle with additional finely chopped cashews.
PER SERVING *150 cal., 9 g fat (5 g sat. fat), 0 g chol., 17 mg sodium, 16 g carb., 1 g fiber, 2 g pro.*

CRANBERRY-CASHEW
CLUSTERS

BANANA-PEANUT FUDGE

Christmas Greetings

Banana-Peanut Fudge

PREP 15 minutes CHILL 2 hours
MAKES 72 servings

   Butter
3 cups white baking pieces
1 14-ounce can sweetened
   condensed milk
¼ cup peanut butter
1 cup chopped peanuts
¾ cup banana chips, chopped or
   broken

1. Line 9×9×2-inch baking pan with foil, extending foil over edges of pan. Butter foil; set pan aside.
2. In heavy 2-quart saucepan cook and stir baking pieces, condensed milk, and peanut butter over low heat until pieces melt and mixture is smooth. Remove saucepan from heat. Stir in ¾ cup of the nuts and banana chips. Spread fudge in prepared pan. Sprinkle with remaining nuts; press lightly into fudge. Cover; chill about 2 hours or until firm.
3. Use foil to lift fudge out of pan. Cut fudge into 1-inch squares. Store, tightly covered, up to 1 week.
PER SERVING *93 cal., 5 g fat (3 g sat. fat), 2 mg chol., 26 mg sodium, 10 g carb., 0 g fiber, 1 g pro.*

Coconut-Macadamia Bark

PREP 22 minutes CHILL 30 minutes
MAKES 20 servings

6 ounces vanilla-flavor candy
   coating, chopped (1 cup)
6 ounces white baking chocolate,
   chopped (1 cup)
1 tablespoon shortening
1½ cups macadamia nuts, chopped
1½ teaspoons finely shredded lime
   peel
¾ cup flaked coconut, toasted*
   Finely shredded lime peel
   (optional)

1. Line a large baking sheet with heavy foil; grease foil. Set aside.
2. In a large microwave-safe bowl combine candy coating, white chocolate, and shortening. Heat, uncovered, on high for 1½ to 2 minutes or until chocolate melts, stirring every 30 seconds. Stir in nuts and lime peel. Pour chocolate mixture onto the prepared baking sheet. Spread mixture evenly in a layer about ¼ inch thick. Sprinkle with the coconut and, if desired, additional lime peel; lightly press into chocolate mixture.
3. Chill candy about 30 minutes or until firm. Use foil to lift candy. Cut or break into pieces.

*Tip To toast coconut, spread it in an even layer in a shallow pan. Bake in a 350°F oven for 5 to 10 minutes, shaking the pan once or twice. Watch closely as coconut can burn quickly.
PER SERVING *187 cal., 14 g fat (6 g sat. fat), 0 mg chol., 15 mg sodium, 14 g carb., 1 g fiber, 1 g pro.*

COCONUT-MACADAMIA BARK

CRACKLIN' CRACKER TOFFEE

Cracklin' Cracker Toffee

PREP **35 minutes**
STAND **1 hour 30 minutes**
MAKES **36 servings**

50 rich rectangular crackers or sesame seed or plain flatbread crackers
1 cup finely crushed graham crackers
1 cup packed brown sugar
½ cup butter
⅓ cup half-and-half or light cream
2 teaspoons vanilla
1½ cups semisweet chocolate pieces
1 tablespoon shortening
1 cup chopped pecans, toasted (see tip, page 25)
½ cup toffee pieces

1. Lightly grease a 15×10×1-inch baking pan; line pan with a single layer of crackers. In a small saucepan combine crushed graham crackers, brown sugar, butter, and half-and-half. Bring to boiling; reduce heat to medium. Cook and stir for 7 minutes. Stir in vanilla. Quickly pour over crackers, spreading evenly. Let stand about 30 minutes or until set.

2. In a small saucepan heat and stir chocolate pieces and shortening over low heat until melted and smooth. Spread evenly over crackers. Immediately, sprinkle with pecans and toffee pieces. Let stand or chill about 1 hour or until set. Cut or break toffee into pieces.

PER SERVING *157 cal., 10 g fat (4 g sat. fat), 10 mg chol., 100 mg sodium, 18 g carb., 1 g fiber, 1 g pro.*

Thin Mint Bark

PREP **20 minutes** CHILL **30 minutes**
MAKES **12 servings**

9 chocolate wafer cookies
6 ounces vanilla-flavor candy coating, chopped (1 cup)
3 ounces milk chocolate pieces (½ cup)
2 teaspoons shortening
3 ounces green mint-flavor baking pieces (½ cup)

1. Line a large baking sheet with heavy foil; grease foil. Arrange cookies in a single layer on the foil.
2. In a medium microwave-safe bowl combine half of the candy coating, the milk chocolate baking pieces, and 1 teaspoon of the shortening. Heat, uncovered, on high for 1 to 1½ minutes or until melted and smooth, stirring every 30 seconds.
3. In a second microwave-safe bowl combine the remaining candy coating, the mint-flavor baking pieces, and the remaining 1 teaspoon shortening. Heat, uncovered, on high for 1 to 1½ minutes or until melted and smooth, stirring every 30 seconds. Drop spoonfuls of milk chocolate and mint mixtures over the cookies, alternating colors and covering the cookies. Using a narrow spatula, swirl the two mixtures together.
4. Chill candy about 30 minutes or until firm. Use foil to lift candy. Cut or break into pieces.

PER SERVING *178 cal., 10 g fat (7 g sat. fat), 4 mg chol., 56 mg sodium, 21 g carb., 0 g fiber, 2 g pro.*

THIN MINT BARK

SEASONED PEPITAS
AND PEANUTS,
PAGE 128

Gifts from the Heart

SPREAD SOME CHEER The best gifts are made by hand and spring from the heart. Beautifully boxed or packaged, these fun holiday foods are easily made in your home kitchen. They are offerings of something good to eat—but also of your time and care.

JUMBO MARSHMALLOW
TREATS

Jumbo Marshmallow Treats

PREP 25 minutes
STAND 8 hours
MAKES 12 servings

⅓ cup butter, cut up
2 10-ounce packages tiny marshmallows
2 13-ounce jars marshmallow creme
1 tablespoon clear vanilla
½ teaspoon salt
15 cups crisp rice cereal
1 cup holiday mix (red/green/white) jimmies or ½ cup colored sugar

1. Line a 13×9×2-inch baking pan with foil, extending foil over edges of the pan. Lightly butter foil; set pan aside.
2. In a heavy 6- to 8-quart Dutch oven melt butter over low heat. Stir in marshmallows. Heat and stir over low heat until melted and smooth. Stir in marshmallow creme, vanilla, and salt until combined. Remove from heat. Reserve 1 cup of the marshmallow mixture. Add cereal to the remaining marshmallow mixture in the Dutch oven; stir gently to coat.
3. Pour cereal mixture into the prepared pan. Using a buttered spatula or buttered waxed paper, press mixture firmly and evenly into pan. Spread the 1 cup reserved marshmallow mixture evenly over top of bars. Sprinkle with jimmies or colored sugar to completely cover. Place a piece of waxed paper on top of the bars. Cover with foil. Place another 13×9×2-pan on the foil and place several heavy items, such as cans or jars of food, in the pan to press the bars. Let stand overnight. Remove pan, foil, and waxed paper. Use foil to lift uncut bars out of pan. Place on a cutting board. Using a long buttered knife, cut into 12 bars.

PER SERVING 601 cal., 9 g fat (3 g sat. fat), 14 mg chol., 367 mg sodium, 132 g carb., 0 g fiber, 4 g pro.

Jumbo Caramel-Pretzel Mallow Treats Prepare as directed, except working quickly, pour half of the cereal mixture into the prepared pan. Press mixture firmly and evenly into pan. Spread the reserved marshmallow mixture evenly over

top. Drop spoonfuls of 1 cup high-quality caramel ice cream topping over bars; spread evenly. Arrange 2 cups miniature chocolate-coated pretzels over caramel sauce. Top with the remaining cereal mixture, pressing evenly into pan.

Jumbo Peanut Butter and Chocolate Treats Prepare Jumbo Caramel-Pretzel Mallow Treats as directed, except omit the caramel topping and, instead, stir ½ cup peanut butter into the reserved marshmallow mixture. Spread peanut butter mixture evenly over top and sprinkle with 1½ cups chopped bittersweet chocolate and ¾ cup chopped dry-roasted peanuts. Top with the remaining cereal mixture, pressing evenly into pan.

Aztec Chocolate Caramel Popcorn

PREP 30 minutes
BAKE 20 minutes at 300°F
MAKES 40 servings

14 cups popped popcorn
1 cup roasted and salted pumpkin seeds (pepitas)*
1½ cups packed brown sugar
¾ cup butter
⅓ cup light-color corn syrup
½ teaspoon baking soda
½ teaspoon vanilla
1 cup semisweet chocolate pieces
1 tablespoon shortening
2 teaspoons ground ancho chile pepper
½ teaspoon instant espresso coffee powder
¼ teaspoon ground cinnamon

1. Preheat oven to 300°F. Remove all unpopped kernels from popped popcorn. Place popcorn and pumpkin seeds into a 17×12×2-inch roasting pan. Keep warm in oven while preparing caramel.
2. Butter a large sheet of foil; set aside. For caramel, in a medium saucepan combine brown sugar, butter, and corn syrup. Cook and stir over medium heat until mixture boils. Continue boiling at a moderate, steady rate, without stirring, for 5 minutes more.
3. Remove saucepan from heat. Stir in baking soda and vanilla. Pour

caramel over popcorn mixture; stir gently to coat. Bake for 15 minutes. Stir mixture; bake for 5 minutes more. Spread popcorn mixture on prepared foil; cool completely.
4. In a small saucepan combine chocolate, shortening, ancho chile pepper, coffee powder, and cinnamon. Cook and stir over low heat until chocolate is melted and smooth.
5. Drizzle chocolate mixture over popcorn mixture; if desired, toss gently to coat. Let stand at room temperature or in the refrigerator until set. Break mixture into clusters. Spoon into gift container.
*To roast raw pumpkin seeds, in a 15×10×1-inch baking pan combine 1 cup raw pumpkin seeds (pepitas), 2 tablespoons olive oil, and ½ teaspoon salt; toss gently to coat. Spread pumpkin seeds in a single layer. Bake in a 350°F oven for 10 minutes, stirring once halfway through baking.

PER SERVING 138 cal., 8 g fat (4 g sat. fat), 9 mg chol., 66 mg sodium, 16 g carb., 1 g fiber, 2 g pro.

AZTEC CHOCOLATE CARAMEL POPCORN

CHUNKY CHOCOLATE AND CHAI BISCOTTI

3. Bake for 25 to 30 minutes or until tops are lightly browned and cracked. Cool on cookie sheet on a wire rack for 15 minutes.
4. Transfer baked loaves to a cutting board. Using a serrated knife, cut each loaf diagonally into ½-inch-thick slices. Place slices flat side down on ungreased cookie sheets. Bake for 8 minutes. Turn slices over; bake 8 to 10 minutes or until crisp and lightly browned. Transfer to wire racks; let cool.
PER SERVING *129 cal., 5 g fat (2 g sat. fat), 28 mg chol., 65 mg sodium, 18 g carb., 1 g fiber, 2 g pro.*

Peanut Butter Cup Cookie Mix

PREP 20 minutes MAKES 40 servings

1¼ cups rolled oats
¾ cup all-purpose flour
½ cup packed brown sugar
¼ cup granulated sugar
½ teaspoon baking powder
⅛ teaspoon baking soda
½ cup coarsely chopped dry-roasted peanuts
1 cup miniature chocolate-covered peanut butter cups, halved

1. In a 1-quart jar layer oats, flour, brown sugar, granulated sugar, baking powder, baking soda, and peanuts. Place peanut butter cups in a plastic bag. Set on top of peanuts in jar. Seal jar; include directions for making cookies.
To Make Cookies Preheat oven to 350°F. Line a cookie sheet with parchment paper or foil. Remove peanut butter cups from jar; set aside. Empty the remaining contents of the jar into a large bowl. In another bowl whisk together ½ cup creamy peanut butter, ¼ cup softened butter, 2 eggs, and ½ teaspoon vanilla. Add to flour mixture; stir until combined. Gently stir in peanut butter cups. Use a ¼-cup measure to drop mounds of dough about 4 inches apart onto cookie sheet. Flatten dough mounds to about ¾ inch thick. Bake for 12 to 14 minutes or until edges are brown. Cool on cookie sheet for 1 minute. Transfer to a wire rack and let cool.
PER SERVING *364 cal., 19 g fat (6 g sat. fat), 45 mg chol., 210 mg sodium, 41 g carb., 3 g fiber, 10 g pro.*

Seasoned Pepitas and Peanuts

(photo page 124)

PREP 15 minutes
BAKE 10 minutes at 350°F
MAKES 16 servings

2 tablespoons butter, melted
1 tablespoon packed brown sugar
1½ teaspoons chili powder
1 teaspoon dried Mexican oregano or dried oregano, crushed
½ teaspoon salt
½ teaspoon ground cumin
½ teaspoon ground coriander
1 cup pumpkin seeds (pepitas)
1 cup Spanish-style peanuts

1. Preheat oven to 350°F. In a small bowl stir together melted butter, brown sugar, chili powder, oregano, salt, cumin, and coriander. Spread pumpkin seeds and peanuts in an even layer in a 15×10×1-inch baking pan. Drizzle with butter mixture; toss to coat.
2. Bake for 10 to 12 minutes or until seeds and nuts are toasted and golden, stirring once halfway through baking. Cool completely. Place mixture in a decorative bag; close bag.
PER SERVING *117 cal., 10 g fat (2 g sat. fat), 4 mg chol., 92 mg sodium, 3 g carb., 2 g fiber, 5 g pro.*

Chunky Chocolate and Chai Biscotti

PREP 45 minutes COOL 15 minutes
BAKE 41 minutes at 325°F
MAKES 30 servings

2¾ cups all-purpose flour
½ cup sugar
¼ cup instant chai latte mix
1½ teaspoons baking powder
1 teaspoon instant espresso coffee powder or instant coffee crystals
¼ teaspoon salt
3 eggs
6 tablespoons butter, melted
1 teaspoon vanilla
1 cup chopped coffee-flavor chocolate bar (about 5.25 ounces)

1. Preheat oven to 325°F. Lightly grease a large cookie sheet; set aside. In a large bowl stir together flour, sugar, latte mix, baking powder, espresso powder, and salt. In a medium bowl whisk together eggs, butter, and vanilla. Add egg mixture to flour mixture and stir until well combined. Stir in chopped chocolate.
2. Divide dough in half. Shape each portion into a 12-inch-long log about 1½ inches in diameter. Place logs about 4 inches apart on the prepared cookie sheet.

PEANUT BUTTER CUP
COOKIE MIX

Peanut Butter Cup
Cookie Mix

CRANBERRY-WHITE
CHOCOLATE CORNMEAL
TEA BISCUITS

Cranberry-White Chocolate Cornmeal Tea Biscuits

PREP 25 minutes
BAKE 9 minutes per batch at 375°F
MAKES 36 servings

Nonstick cooking spray
½ cup dried cranberries, coarsely chopped
1½ cups all-purpose flour
½ cup yellow cornmeal
¼ cup packed brown sugar
1½ teaspoons baking powder
¼ teaspoon baking soda
¼ teaspoon salt
¼ cup butter
4 ounces white baking chocolate (with cocoa butter), chopped
1 egg white, lightly beaten
1 8-ounce carton light sour cream
3 tablespoons fat-free milk

1. Preheat oven to 375°F. Coat a cookie sheet with nonstick spray or line with parchment paper; set aside. Place cranberries in a bowl; add enough boiling water to cover. Let stand for 5 minutes; drain well. Meanwhile, in a bowl combine flour, cornmeal, brown sugar, baking powder, baking soda, and salt. Using a pastry blender, cut in butter until mixture resembles coarse crumbs. Stir in drained cranberries and white chocolate. Make a well in the center of the flour mixture.
2. In a bowl combine egg white, sour cream, and milk. Add egg white mixture all at once to flour mixture. Using a fork, stir until combined. Drop dough by well-rounded teaspoons 2 inches apart onto prepared cookie sheet.
3. Bake for 9 to 11 minutes or until edges are lightly browned and tops are set. Transfer biscuits to wire racks and let cool. Affix a strip of patterned paper around the side of a cookie tin. Glue ribbon around the edge of the lid. Attach a circle of solid paper to the top of the lid; layer two smaller circles on top. Add your personal decorative touches. Fill the tin with tea biscuits.
PER SERVING *75 cal., 3 g fat (2 g sat. fat), 6 mg chol., 55 mg sodium, 10 g carb., 0 g fiber, 1 g pro.*

Snowflake Mix

PREP 20 minutes COOL 1 hour
MAKES 16 servings

3 cups bite-size rice square cereal
3 cups bite-size corn square cereal
1 cup small pretzel twists or pretzel sticks
1 cup honey-roasted peanuts
1 12-ounce package white baking pieces
1 12-ounce package mint-flavor candy-coated milk chocolate pieces

1. In a very large bowl combine cereals, pretzels, and peanuts; set aside.
2. Melt white baking pieces according to package directions. Pour over cereal mixture. Stir gently to coat. Spread cereal mixture on a large piece of waxed paper or parchment paper. Sprinkle with chocolate pieces. Cool completely and break into pieces. Place mix in a decorative bag; close bag.
PER SERVING *437 cal., 20 g fat (14 g sat. fat), 3 mg chol., 241 mg sodium, 56 g carb., 1 g fiber, 3 g pro.*

Caramel-Mocha Dessert Sauce

PREP 5 minutes COOK 10 minutes
MAKES 12 servings

12 vanilla caramels, unwrapped
⅔ cup whipping cream
1 tablespoon instant coffee crystals
1½ ounces white baking chocolate, chopped
5 ounces dark or bittersweet chocolate, chopped

1. In a small saucepan combine caramels and whipping cream. Heat over medium-low heat until melted and smooth, stirring frequently. Add coffee crystals, white chocolate, and dark chocolate; stir until smooth. Remove from heat and cool completely. Transfer to jar; cover. Refrigerate. Tie a ribbon with gift tag around the rim of the jar.
PER SERVING *162 cal., 12 g fat (7 g sat. fat), 19 mg chol., 29 mg sodium, 15 g carb., 1 g fiber, 2 g pro.*

Shaker-Style Meyer Lemon Pie

PREP 45 minutes **CHILL** overnight
BAKE 1 hour at 350°F
COOL 10 minutes **MAKES** 8 servings

    4 Meyer lemons or lemons
  2¼ cups sugar
    2 tablespoons all-purpose flour
    ¼ teaspoon salt
    5 eggs
    ⅓ cup milk
    ¼ cup butter, melted
    1 recipe Pastry for Single-Crust Pie
    1 recipe Candied Lemon Slices
       (optional)

1. Finely shred enough of the peel from 2 of the lemons to measure 2 tablespoons. Juice 1 or 2 of the lemons to measure ¼ cup juice. Cover and chill juice and peel. Peel the remaining 2 lemons, cutting away any white pith; discard peels. Very thinly slice lemons crosswise. Remove and discard seeds. Pour ½ cup of the sugar into a medium bowl. Top with lemon slices; sprinkle with another ½ cup of the sugar to cover completely. If necessary, toss gently to coat. Cover and chill overnight.
2. Preheat oven to 350°F. For filling, in a large bowl combine the remaining 1¼ cups sugar, the flour, and salt. In a bowl whisk together the eggs, milk, butter, and the reserved lemon juice and lemon peel. Add egg mixture to flour mixture; stir until combined. Fold in chilled lemon slice-sugar mixture.
3. Prepare and roll out Pastry for Single-Crust Pie. Pour filling into pastry-lined plate. To prevent overbrowning, line edge of pie with foil.
4. Bake for 20 minutes. Remove foil. Bake about 40 minutes more or until evenly puffed and light brown (filling will still be jiggly). Cool completely on a wire rack. Cover and chill within 2 hours. If desired top pie with Candied Lemon Slices.

Pastry for Single-Crust Pie In a medium bowl stir together 1½ cups all-purpose flour and ½ teaspoon salt. Using a pastry blender, cut in ¼ cup shortening and ¼ cup butter, cut up, until pieces are pea size. Sprinkle 1 tablespoon ice water over part of the flour mixture; toss gently with a fork. Push moistened pastry to side of bowl. Repeat moistening flour mixture, using 1 tablespoon ice water at a time, until all of the flour mixture is moistened (¼ to ⅓ cup ice water total). Gather flour mixture into a ball, kneading gently until it holds together. On a lightly floured surface use your hands to slightly flatten pastry. Roll pastry from center edges into a circle about 12 inches in diameter. Wrap pastry circle around the rolling pin. Unroll into a 9-inch pie plate. Ease into pie plate without stretching it. Trim pastry to ½ inch beyond edge of pie plate. Fold under extra pastry even with the plate's edge. Crimp edge as desired. Do not prick pastry.

PER SERVING 478 cal., 16 g fat (9 g sat. fat), 164 mg chol., 350 mg sodium, 83 g carb., 3 g fiber, 8 g pro.

Candied Lemon Slices Slice 2 Meyer lemons or lemons into ¼-inch slices. Remove seeds. Roll slices in sugar (about ½ cup) to coat well. Coat an extra-large skillet with nonstick cooking spray. Heat skillet over medium-high heat. Arrange lemon slices in a single layer in skillet. Cook for 3 to 4 minutes on each side or until sugar dissolves and lemon slices appear glazed (do not let brown). Transfer to a piece of foil; cool completely. Roll cooled slices in sugar again before using.

Ginger-Date Pumpkin Loaves

PREP 25 minutes
BAKE 35 minutes at 350°F
COOL 10 minutes **STAND** overnight
MAKES 36 servings

    1 cup all-purpose flour
    1 cup whole wheat flour
    1 cup granulated sugar
    1 tablespoon finely chopped
       crystallized ginger
  2½ teaspoons baking powder
    ½ teaspoon baking soda
    ½ teaspoon ground nutmeg
    ¼ teaspoon salt
    1 cup canned pumpkin
    ½ cup milk
    2 eggs
    ⅓ cup shortening
    1 8-ounce package chopped pitted
       dates
    1 recipe Spiced Glaze
       Crystallized ginger, finely
       chopped (optional)

1. Preheat oven to 350°F. Lightly grease bottoms and halfway up the sides of five 4½×2½×1½-inch loaf pans.
2. In a mixing bowl stir together all-purpose flour, whole wheat flour, granulated sugar, the 1 tablespoon ginger, baking powder, baking soda, nutmeg, and salt. Add pumpkin, milk, eggs, and shortening. Beat with an electric mixer on low to medium for 30 seconds. Beat on high for 2 minutes, scraping sides of bowl occasionally. Stir in dates. Spoon the batter into pans.
3. Bake for 35 to 40 minutes or until a wooden toothpick inserted near centers comes out clean. Cool in pans on wire racks for 10 minutes. Remove from pans; cool completely on wire racks. Wrap and store overnight before slicing.
4. Before giving as gifts, drizzle with Spiced Glaze. If desired sprinkle with additional chopped crystallized ginger. Let stand until glaze is set.

Spiced Glaze In a small bowl stir together 1 cup powdered sugar and ¼ teaspoon ground ginger. Stir in enough water (4 to 6 teaspoons) until glaze reaches drizzling consistency.

PER SERVING 148 cal., 3 g fat (1 g sat. fat), 15 mg chol., 94 mg sodium, 28 g carb., 2 g fiber, 2 g pro.

GINGER-DATE
PUMPKIN LOAVES

APPLE CIDER- AND GINGER-
BRINED TURKEY, PAGE 141

Ringing In the New Year

START FRESH Celebrate the promise of a new beginning with a festive feast for friends and family. Whether it's a sit-down dinner or a spread of appetizers and desserts, you'll find food for good times and good luck here.

THAI TURKEY
MEATBALLS

Thai Turkey Meatballs

PREP 10 minutes
SLOW COOK 2½ hours (low) or
1½ hours (high)
MAKES 12 servings

- 1 13.5-ounce can unsweetened coconut milk
- 3 tablespoons peanut butter
- 2 tablespoons soy sauce
- 2 tablespoons lime juice
- 1 to 2 tablespoons chile paste
- 2 cloves garlic, minced
- 2 14-ounce packages frozen home-style turkey meatballs, thawed
- ½ cup coarsely chopped dry-roasted peanuts
- ⅓ cup snipped fresh cilantro

1. In a 4-quart slow cooker combine coconut milk, peanut butter, soy sauce, lime juice, chile paste, and garlic. Stir in meatballs. Cover and cook on low-heat heat setting for 2½ to 3 hours or on high-heat setting for 1½ to 2 hours.
2. Using a slotted spoon, carefully transfer meatballs to a shallow bowl or rimmed platter. Place a toothpick in each meatball. Spoon the remaining cooking liquid around meatballs; sprinkle with chopped peanuts and cilantro.
PER SERVING 257 cal., 17 g fat (8 g sat. fat), 39 mg chol., 641 mg sodium, 8 g carb., 2 g fiber, 20 g pro.

Lemony Artichoke Dip

PREP 25 minutes
SLOW COOK 2 hours (low)
MAKES 32 servings

- 1 tablespoon olive oil
- 1 cup chopped fresh mushrooms
- ¼ cup chopped red sweet pepper
- 3 tablespoons finely chopped shallot
- 1 clove garlic, minced
- 1 8-ounce carton sour cream
- ½ cup original cream cheese for cooking
- 1 teaspoon finely shredded lemon peel
- 1 tablespoon lemon juice
- 1 tablespoon Dijon mustard
- 3 6-ounce jars marinated artichoke hearts, drained and coarsely chopped
- 1 cup shredded Gruyère or Swiss cheese (4 ounces)
   Toasted baguette-style French bread slices or pita chips

1. In a medium skillet heat oil over medium heat. Add mushrooms, sweet pepper, shallot, and garlic; cook mixture until pepper and shallot are tender, stirring frequently.
2. In a medium bowl combine sour cream, cream cheese for cooking,
lemon peel, lemon juice, and mustard. Stir in mushroom mixture, artichoke hearts, and Gruyère cheese. Spoon artichoke mixture into a 1½- or 2-quart slow cooker.
3. Cover and cook on low-heat setting for 2 to 2½ hours or until heated through. Serve immediately or keep warm, covered, on warm or low-heat setting for up to 2 hours. Stir before serving. Serve with toasted bread slices or pita chips.
PER SERVING 71 cal., 6 g fat (2 g sat. fat), 9 mg chol., 105 mg sodium, 2 g carb., 0 g fiber, 2 g pro.

Two Tomato Bruschetta

PREP 10 minutes
BAKE 5 minutes at 350°F
MAKES 4 servings

- ⅓ cup crumbled feta cheese with tomato and basil
- ⅓ cup dried tomatoes (not oil-packed), chopped
- 2 tablespoons snipped fresh basil
- 2 tablespoons snipped fresh parsley
- 2 tablespoons olive oil
- 1 clove garlic, minced
- ¼ teaspoon freshly ground black pepper
- 8 to 10 slices whole grain baguette (each about ½ inch thick)
- 2 roma tomatoes, thinly sliced

1. Preheat oven to 350°F. In a small bowl combine feta cheese, dried tomatoes, basil, and parsley. Set aside.
2. In another small bowl stir together oil, garlic, and pepper. Brush oil mixture evenly over bread slices. Place bread slices on a large baking sheet. Bake about 5 minutes or until lightly toasted. Remove from oven. Top with tomato slices. Spoon feta cheese mixture on top of tomato slices. Serve immediately or broil 3 to 4 inches from the heat for 1 to 2 minutes or until cheese is slightly melted.
PER SERVING 181 cal., 11 g fat (2 g sat. fat), 8 mg chol., 344 mg sodium, 18 g carb., 2 g fiber, 6 g pro.

TWO TOMATO
BRUSCHETTA

CITRUS CIDER

Citrus Cider

PREP 10 minutes
SLOW COOK 5 hours (low) or
2½ hours (high)
MAKES 13 servings

2   quarts (8 cups) apple cider or
    apple juice
1   cup orange juice*
½   cup lemon juice*
¼   cup honey
8   inches stick cinnamon, broken
8   whole cloves
3   slices fresh ginger

1. In a 3½- or 4-quart slow cooker combine cider, orange juice, lemon juice, and honey. Stir to dissolve honey.
2. For the spice bag, cut a 6- to 8-inch square from a double thickness of 100%-cotton cheesecloth. Place cinnamon, cloves, and ginger in center of cheesecloth. Bring up the corners; tie closed with 100%-cotton kitchen string. Add spice bag to slow cooker.
3. Cover and cook on low-heat setting for 5 to 6 hours or on high-heat setting for 2½ to 3 hours. Discard spice bag.

*If you squeeze fresh oranges and lemons for the juice, use a vegetable peeler to cut several wide strips of peel from the fruit, avoiding the white pith underneath. Add the peel to the spice bag.

PER SERVING *89 cal., 0 g fat, 0 mg. chol., 1 mg sodium, 10 g carb., 0 g fiber, 0 g pro.*

Spanish Chorizo, Date, and Manchego-Stuffed Pork Loin

PREP 50 minutes
ROAST 20 minutes at 450°F/1 hour
at 325°F STAND 15 minutes
MAKES 10 servings

15 to 16 ounces uncooked chorizo
    sausage
¾   cup chopped onion
½   cup bottled roasted piquillo
    peppers or sweet peppers,
    chopped
2   cloves garlic, minced
1   teaspoon fresh thyme leaves
½   cup Marcona almonds, coarsely
    chopped
¼   cup chopped pitted dates
1   4- to 5-pound boneless pork top
    loin roast (single loin)
½   teaspoon salt
½   teaspoon black pepper
¼   teaspoon smoked paprika
1   cup coarsely shredded
    Manchego cheese (4 ounces)
10 slices bacon

1. Preheat oven to 450°F. If sausage is in links, remove casings. In a large skillet cook sausage over medium heat for 3 to 4 minutes, using a wooden spoon to break up meat as it cooks. Add onion, roasted peppers, garlic, and thyme; cook and stir for 10 minutes more. Drain off fat. Stir in almonds and dates; set aside.
2. Trim fat from pork. Butterfly pork by making a lengthwise cut down the center of the meat, cutting to within ½ inch of the other side. Spread open. Place knife in the V of the cut. Cut horizontally to the cut surface and away from the center cut to within ½ inch of the other side of the meat. Repeat on opposite side of the V. Spread meat open. Cover meat with plastic wrap. Working from center (thicker part) to edges, pound with a meat mallet until ½ to ¾ inch thick. Remove plastic wrap.
3. Sprinkle pork with salt, black pepper, and smoked paprika. Spread sausage mixture over one side of pork; sprinkle sausage mixture with cheese. Starting with the filled side, roll pork into a spiral.
4. On a sheet of waxed paper arrange bacon slices vertically with long sides touching. Place pork in center of the bacon. Use the waxed paper to lift the bacon and wrap it around the pork. Tie at 2-inch intervals with heavy 100%-cotton kitchen string. Place pork on a rack in a shallow roasting pan. Insert an oven-going meat thermometer into center of meat.
5. Roast, uncovered, for 20 minutes. Reduce oven temperature to 325°F and roast for about 1 hour or until thermometer registers 145°F.
6. Transfer pork to a cutting board. Cover loosely with foil; let stand for 15 minutes.

PER SERVING *750 cal., 53 g fat (19 g sat. fat), 187 mg chol., 1,202 mg sodium, 8 g carb., 1 g fiber, 57 g pro.*

SPANISH CHORIZO,
DATE, AND MANCHEGO-
STUFFED PORK LOIN

ORZO WITH
BUTTERNUT SQUASH,
SAGE, AND BACON

Orzo with Butternut Squash, Sage, and Bacon

START TO FINISH 35 minutes
MAKES 8 servings

4½ cups chicken broth
8 ounces dried orzo pasta (rosamarina)
6 slices bacon, chopped
1½ cups chopped onions (3 medium)
1 tablespoon snipped fresh sage
3 cloves garlic, minced
4 cups peeled and chopped butternut squash

1. In a large saucepan bring 4 cups of the broth to boiling. Stir in orzo. Cook about 8 minutes or until tender; drain. Return orzo to hot pan; cover.
2. Meanwhile, in a 4-quart Dutch oven cook bacon over medium heat until crisp. Remove bacon with a slotted spoon and drain on paper towels, reserving 2 tablespoons drippings in Dutch oven.
3. Add onions to the reserved drippings; cook about 4 minutes or until tender. Add sage and garlic; cook and stir for 1 minute. Add squash and remaining ½ cup broth. Bring to boiling; reduce heat. Simmer, covered, for 10 to 15 minutes or until squash is tender. Cook, uncovered, until most of the liquid is evaporated, stirring occasionally. Stir in cooked orzo and bacon.

PER SERVING 220 cal., 7 g fat (2 g sat. fat), 11 mg chol., 690 mg sodium, 33 g carb., 3 g fiber, 8 g pro.

Apple Cider- and Ginger-Brined Turkey

PREP 20 minutes CHILL 24 hours
COOK 5 minutes
ROAST 2 hours 45 minutes at 325°F
STAND 15 minutes
MAKES 12 servings

5½ cups apple cider
1 cup finely chopped fresh ginger*
¾ cup kosher salt
½ cup packed brown sugar
3 bay leaves
2 2×1-inch strips orange peel
1 tablespoon whole black peppercorns
4 whole cloves

APPLE CIDER- AND
GINGER-BRINED
TURKEY

12 cups ice water**
1 8- to 10-pound fresh or frozen turkey, thawed if frozen
1 recipe Cider Sauce

1. For brine, in a large stockpot combine apple cider, ginger, salt, brown sugar, bay leaves, orange peel, peppercorns, and cloves. Bring to boiling; reduce heat. Simmer for 5 minutes; cool slightly. Stir in ice the water. (If all of the ice water doesn't fit in the pot, add the remainder to turkey in the brining bag.)***
2. Remove neck and giblets from turkey; discard. Rinse turkey; pat dry with paper towels. Place turkey in a large brining or roasting bag set in a large bowl or plastic tub. Add enough brine to cover turkey; seal bag. Chill for 24 to 36 hours.
3. Preheat oven to 325°F. Remove turkey from brine; discard brine. Pat turkey dry with paper towels. Tuck drumstick ends under band of skin across tail, if available. If there is no band of skin, tie drumsticks securely to the tail using 100%-cotton kitchen string. Twist wing tips under back.
4. Place turkey, breast side up, on a rack in a shallow roasting pan. Insert an oven-going meat thermometer into the center of an inside thigh muscle. The thermometer should not touch bone. Cover turkey loosely with foil.
5. Roast for 2¼ hours. Remove foil; cut band of skin or string between drumsticks so thighs will cook evenly. Roast for 30 to 45 minutes more or

until the thermometer registers 175°F. (The juices should run clear and drumsticks should move easily in their sockets.) Remove from oven.
6. Cover turkey with foil; let stand for 15 to 20 minutes before carving. Transfer turkey to a cutting board. Carve turkey. Serve turkey with Cider Sauce.

Cider Sauce In a medium saucepan bring 4 cups apple cider to boiling; reduce heat. Simmer, uncovered, for 20 to 30 minutes or until cider is reduced by half (2 cups). In a small bowl combine 2 tablespoons cold water and 2 teaspoons cornstarch; stir into cider. Cook and stir over medium heat until slightly thickened and bubbly. Stir in ¼ cup butter, 1 teaspoon grated fresh ginger, and 1 teaspoon finely shredded orange peel.

*To chop the ginger with ease, peel about a 4-inch piece of fresh ginger and cut into pieces. Place in a food processor, cover, and process with on/off turns until finely chopped.
**For ice water, fill a glass measuring cup with ice, then add the water. Repeat as needed until you reach 12 cups total.
***If you have a stockpot large enough to fit the bird that will also fit into the refrigerator, go ahead and use the pot instead of the brining bag.

PER SERVING 543 cal., 25 g fat (9 g sat. fat), 197 mg chol., 1,498 mg sodium, 14 g carb., 0 g fiber, 56 g pro.

Quinoa with Roasted Beets and Chive Vinaigrette

PREP 25 minutes COOK 15 minutes
ROAST 40 minutes at 400°F
STAND 15 minutes
MAKES 6 servings

 1½ pounds baby beets
  4 cloves garlic, peeled
  4 tablespoons olive oil
  ¼ teaspoon salt
  ¼ teaspoon black pepper
  3 cups water
 1½ cups quinoa, rinsed and drained
  ¼ teaspoon salt
  3 tablespoons white balsamic vinegar or white wine vinegar
  1 tablespoon snipped fresh chives
  1 teaspoon Dijon mustard
     Salt
     Ground black pepper
  ¾ cup crumbled ricotta salata or feta cheese
  ⅓ cup chopped walnuts, toasted (see tip, page 25)
  1 shallot, thinly sliced
     Snipped fresh chives

1. Preheat oven to 400°F. Cut tops off beets and trim root ends. Halve or quarter beets. Place beets and garlic in a 15×10×1-inch baking pan. Drizzle with 1 tablespoon of the oil and sprinkle with ¼ teaspoon salt and ¼ teaspoon pepper; toss to coat. Cover with foil.
2. Roast for 40 to 45 minutes or until beets are tender. Let stand, covered, for 15 minutes. To remove skins, wrap beets, one at a time, in a paper towel and gently rub to remove skins. (If skins are very tender, you do not need to remove them.) Mash garlic and set aside.
3. Meanwhile, in a medium saucepan combine the water, quinoa, and ¼ teaspoon salt. Bring to boiling; reduce heat. Simmer, covered, about 15 minutes or until liquid is absorbed.
4. For vinaigrette, in a screw-top jar combine the remaining 3 tablespoons oil, the vinegar, the 1 tablespoon chives, and the mustard. Season to taste with salt and pepper.
5. In a medium bowl combine cooked quinoa, the vinaigrette, cheese, walnuts, and shallot. Toss to combine.
6. Divide quinoa mixture among serving plates. Top with roasted beets. Sprinkle with additional snipped chives. Serve warm or at room temperature.
PER SERVING *364 cal., 19 g fat (2 g sat. fat), 13 mg chol., 521 mg sodium, 38 g carb., 6 g fiber, 11 g pro.*

Broccolini with Peas and Seared Lemons

PREP 25 minutes COOK 6 minutes
MAKES 12 servings

  2 pounds Broccolini, trimmed
  8 ounces Swiss chard, trimmed and cut into 2- to 3-inch lengths
  1 cup frozen peas
  2 tablespoons butter
  1 lemon, thinly sliced
  ¼ cup chicken broth
  ¼ teaspoon crushed red pepper
  ¼ cup chives
  ½ teaspoon coarse salt

1. Bring a 6- to 8-quart pot of salted water to a boil. Add Broccolini, cook for 2 minutes and then add Swiss chard and peas. Simmer, covered, for 4 minutes or until bright green. Drain. Meanwhile, melt butter in a large skillet. Add lemon slices and cook over medium to medium-high heat until lemons are soft and browned and butter is browned, 3 minutes each side. (Do not move lemons around too much so that they will get a nice sear.) Return the drained Broccolini, Swiss chard, and peas to the pot. Add the broth and crushed red pepper to the pan and toss gently. Transfer the Broccolini mixture to a serving platter and top with the lemons. Top with chives and coarse salt before serving.
PER SERVING *48 cal., 2 g fat (1 g sat. fat), 5 mg chol., 186 mg sodium, 6 g carb., 2 g fiber, 2 g pro.*

Vegetables Romesco

PREP 30 minutes
ROAST 25 minutes at 425°F
MAKES 10 servings

  3 medium zucchini, cut into ½-inch slices (1½ pounds)
  3 medium yellow summer squash, cut into ½-inch slices (about 1 pound)
  1 large red onion, cut into ½-inch wedges
  3 tablespoons olive oil
  ½ teaspoon kosher salt
  ½ teaspoon freshly ground black pepper
  1 recipe Romesco Sauce

1. Preheat oven to 425°F. In a large roasting pan combine zucchini, yellow squash, and red onion. Drizzle with oil and sprinkle with salt and pepper; toss gently to coat. Spread vegetables in an even layer.
2. Roast, uncovered, for 25 to 30 minutes or until vegetables are tender and brown on the edges.
3. Transfer vegetables to a serving platter. Drizzle with Romesco Sauce.
Romesco Sauce In a food processor combine ¼ cup toasted slivered almonds, ¼ cup soft bread crumbs, 1 clove garlic, and ¼ teaspoon salt. Cover and process with several on/off pulses until almonds are finely chopped. Add 1 cup roasted red sweet peppers, ½ cup seeded and chopped tomato (1 medium), 3 tablespoons olive oil, 4 teaspoons sherry vinegar, ½ teaspoon smoked paprika, and ¼ teaspoon crushed red pepper. Cover and process until mixture is smooth.
PER SERVING *119 cal., 10 g fat (1 g sat. fat), 0 g chol., 171 mg sodium, 8 g carb., 2 g fiber, 2 g pro.*

QUINOA WITH ROASTED BEETS AND CHIVE VINAIGRETTE

VEGETABLES
ROMESCO

ROASTED PEAR AND
CLEMENTINE SALAD

Roasted Pear and Clementine Salad

PREP 40 minutes
ROAST 25 minutes at 425°F
CHILL 30 minutes   MAKES 8 servings

- 3 tablespoons white balsamic or white wine vinegar
- 2 tablespoons olive oil
- ¼ teaspoon salt
- ¼ teaspoon black pepper
- 3 large firm, ripe Anjou or Bosc pears, peeled, cored, and cut into 8 wedges each (about 1½ pounds total)
- 1 recipe Clementine-Balsamic Salad Dressing
- 3 medium clementines, or oranges, peeled and separated into segments
- 4 large heads butterhead (Boston or Bibb) lettuce
- ½ cup coarsely chopped pistachio nuts, or slivered almonds, toasted (see tip, page 25)
- 3 ounces Gorgonzola or other blue cheese, or soft goat cheese (chèvre), crumbled

1. Preheat oven to in a 425°F. In a small bowl combine vinegar, oil, salt, and black pepper. Gently toss pear wedges with vinegar/oil and spread in a shallow baking pan. Roast, uncovered, for 25 to 30 minutes or until pears are tender and beginning to brown, turning pears twice. Remove pan from oven and set on a wire rack to cool. Lift pears from juices; discard liquid.
2. Prepare Clementine-Balsamic Salad Dressing; transfer to a medium bowl. Gently stir clementine segments into dressing. Cover and chill in the refrigerator for at least 30 minutes.
3. To serve, remove 16 outer leaves of lettuce and set aside. Shred remaining lettuce by slicing into ¼-inch strips. Arrange reserved lettuce leaves on eight chilled salad plates. Top each with a mound of shredded lettuce. Divide dressing among the salads; top with pear wedges and pistachio nuts. Sprinkle with Gorgonzola.
Clementine-Balsamic Dressing Salad In a blender combine ⅓ cup balsamic or white wine vinegar; 1 teaspoon finely shredded clementine or orange peel; ¼ cup clementine or orange juice; 2 teaspoons sugar; 1 teaspoon honey Dijon mustard; ½ teaspoon dried thyme; ¼ teaspoon salt; dash cayenne pepper; and 1 clove garlic, minced. Cover and blend until smooth. With blender running, slowing add ¾ cup olive oil in a thin, steady stream until dressing reaches desired consistency. Makes 1 cup.
PER SERVING *382 cal., 30 g fat (6 g sat. fat), 8 mg chol., 307 mg sodium, 25 g carb., 5 g fiber, 5 g pro.*

CLASSIC OYSTER STEW

Classic Oyster Stew

START TO FINISH 25 minutes
MAKES 10 servings

- 3 ounces shucked oysters, undrained (about 1 pound)
- 4 cups whole milk
- 2 cups whipping cream
- 7 tablespoons unsalted butter
- 1 cup finely chopped yellow onion
- ½ cup finely chopped celery (1 stalk)
- ¾ teaspoon kosher salt
- 3 tablespoons all-purpose flour
  Dash cayenne pepper
  Snipped fresh parsley

1. Drain oysters, reserving liquor. Remove any shell pieces. Set aside.
2. In medium saucepan heat milk and cream just to simmering; keep warm.
3. In a Dutch oven heat 4 tablespoons of the butter over medium heat. When butter is melted and bubbling, add onion, celery, and ½ teaspoon of the salt, stirring well to coat in butter. Cook slowly, about 10 minutes, stirring often until onion is tender and translucent. Sprinkle flour over vegetable mixture. Cook 2 minutes more, stirring well to blend in the flour. Slowly whisk in the hot milk and cream; ring mixture back to a low simmer, stirring occasionally.
4. Meanwhile, in a large nonstick skillet heat remaining 3 tablespoons butter over medium heat until hot and bubbly. Add drained oysters in a single layer. Sprinkle with remaining salt and a few grinds of black pepper. Cook just until oysters begin to curl around the edges and gills are slightly exposed. Transfer oysters to the milk mixture in Dutch oven. Turn off heat.
5. Add oyster liquor to hot skillet. Cook 2 to 3 minutes, until boiling. Immediately transfer to stew in Dutch oven; stir. Stir in cayenne pepper. Cover and let stand for 10 minutes. Sprinkle servings with parsley.
PER SERVING *342 cal., 30 g fat (18 g sat. fat), 121 mg chol., 303 mg sodium, 11 g carb., 0 g fiber, 8 g pro.*

CREME BRU-LATTE

Creme Bru-latte

PREP 15 minutes
BAKE 40 minutes at 325°F
COOL 4 hours STAND 20 minutes
BROIL 4 minutes MAKES 8 servings

8 egg yolks
⅔ cup sugar
3½ cups half-and-half or light cream
1 tablespoon instant espresso powder
2 tablespoons coffee liqueur or strong brewed coffee
⅓ cup turbinado sugar

1. Preheat oven to 325°F. In a medium bowl combine egg yolks and sugar. Whisk until combined.
2. In a small saucepan combine half-and-half and espresso powder; heat just to a boil. Gradually whisk hot cream mixture into yolk mixture. Stir in liqueur. Pour mixture evenly into eight 6-ounce ramekins or oven-safe mugs.
3. Place ramekins in two 13×9×2-inch baking pans. Pour enough boiling water into the pans to reach halfway up the sides of the ramekins.
4. Bake about 40 minutes or until centers appear nearly set when lightly shaken. Carefully remove pans from oven. Remove ramekins from water; cool on a wire rack. Cover and chill for at least 4 hours or overnight.

5. Before serving, let custards stand at room temperature for 20 minutes. Sprinkle custards evenly with turbinado sugar. Place on a baking sheet. Caramelize sugar with a culinary torch or broil 4 to 5 inches from heat.* Serve immediately.
*Choose the culinary torch if your dishes are not broiler-safe.

PER SERVING *304 cal., 17 g fat (9 g sat. fat), 224 mg chol., 52 mg sodium, 33 g carb., 0 g fiber, 6 g pro.*

Dark Chocolate Cake with Coconut Macaroon Filling

PREP 40 minutes STAND 30 minutes
BAKE 1 hour at 325°F
COOL 15 minutes
MAKES 12 servings

¾ cup butter
3 eggs
1 tablespoon unsweetened cocoa powder
1¾ cups all-purpose flour
1 teaspoon baking soda
½ teaspoon salt
4 ounces dark chocolate, chopped
⅓ cup bourbon or water
1 recipe Coconut Macaroon Filling
1 cup granulated sugar
¾ cup packed brown sugar
1½ teaspoons vanilla
Powdered sugar (optional)
Unsweetened cocoa powder (optional)

1. Allow butter and eggs to stand at room temperature for 30 minutes. Meanwhile, grease a 10-inch fluted tube pan. Add 1 tablespoon cocoa powder. Shake and tilt pan to coat bottom, sides, and tube; shake out any excess cocoa powder. Set pan aside. In a medium bowl stir together flour, baking soda, and salt; set aside.
2. In a small microwave-safe bowl heat dark chocolate on high for 1 to 2 minutes or until melted, stirring every 30 seconds. Cool slightly. Place bourbon in a 2-cup glass measuring cup; add enough cold water to measure 1¼ cups liquid; set aside.
3. Preheat oven to 325°F. Prepare Coconut Macaroon Filling; set aside. In a large mixing bowl beat butter with an electric mixer on medium to high for 30 seconds. Add granulated sugar and brown sugar. Beat until combined, scraping sides of bowl occasionally. Add eggs, one at a time, beating well after each addition. Beat in melted chocolate and vanilla. Alternately add flour mixture and bourbon mixture to chocolate mixture, beating on low after each addition just until combined. Spoon half of the batter into the prepared pan, spreading evenly. Drop Coconut Macaroon Filling by rounded teaspoons onto batter in pan, avoiding the edges. Top with the remaining batter.
4. Bake about 1 hour or until a wooden toothpick inserted near the center comes out clean. Cool in pan on a wire rack for 15 minutes. Remove cake from pan; cool completely on wire rack. If desired, sprinkle cake lightly with powdered sugar and additional cocoa powder.
Coconut Macaroon Filling In a medium mixing bowl beat 1 egg white with an electric mixer on medium until soft peaks form (tips curl). Gradually add ¼ cup sugar, beating on high until stiff peaks form (tips stand straight). Fold in 1 cup flaked coconut, 1 tablespoon all-purpose flour, and 1 teaspoon vanilla.

PER SERVING *440 cal., 19 g fat (13 g sat. fat), 78 mg chol., 359 mg sodium, 59 g carb., 2 g fiber, 5 g pro.*

Resolving to have a good time on New Year's Eve is as easy as inviting good friends over for fabulous food and celebration.

DARK CHOCOLATE CAKE
WITH COCONUT
MACAROON FILLING

APPLE-BRANDY PIES,
PAGE 155

Company's Coming

SIMPLE BUT SPECIAL When you have overnight guests this season, keep meals easygoing to save energy for all of the other holiday preparations. These recipes are perfect for casual, relaxed company meals. It's fabulous food without the fuss.

Prosciutto-Wrapped Asparagus Panini

PREP 25 minutes   COOK 4 minutes
MAKES 4 servings

16 asparagus spears (12 ounces)
8 very thin prosciutto slices (5 ounces)
8 slices marble rye bread
1 tablespoon coarse ground mustard
1 cup lightly packed arugula (optional)
8 thin slices provolone cheese
1 tablespoon bottled balsamic vinaigrette (or 2 teaspoons olive oil combined with 1 teaspoon balsamic vinegar)

1. Snap off and discard woody bases from asparagus. Trim stalks barely longer than the bread slices. Place a steamer rack in the bottom of a large saucepan and add water to just below the basket. Bring to boiling. Add asparagus. Cover and reduce heat. Steam for 3 to 5 minutes or until crisp-tender. Transfer asparagus to a bowl of ice water for 30 seconds to cool; drain.
2. Using kitchen scissors, cut each piece of prosciutto in half lengthwise. Starting at the base of an asparagus spear, wrap 1 halved prosciutto piece around the asparagus spear diagonally to the top of the spear. Repeat with remaining asparagus and prosciutto.
3. Spread 4 slices of the bread with mustard. Place 4 prosciutto-wrapped asparagus spears horizontally on each mustard-topped bread slice. If desired, top with arugula. Add 2 slices of cheese to each sandwich, arranging slices to completely cover bread. Brush the remaining 4 bread slices lightly with balsamic vinaigrette. Place bread, vinaigrette sides down, on top of cheese.
4. Preheat a panini press; place sandwiches (half at a time if necessary) in grill. Cover and cook for 4 to 5 minutes or until cheese melts. (Or place sandwiches in preheated grill pan or skillet. Weight sandwiches down with another skillet with a few unopened cans of food inside. Grill about 3 minutes or until bread is toasted. Turn sandwiches over, weight them down, and grill until second side is toasted, 2 to 3 minutes.)

PER SERVING 402 cal., 15 g fat (8 g sat. fat), 54 mg chol., 1,713 mg sodium, 39 g carb., 4 g fiber, 29 g pro.

Meatball Pie

PREP 30 minutes   COOK 20 minutes
BAKE 1 hour at 350°F
STAND 15 minutes   MAKES 8 servings

3 eggs, lightly beaten
⅔ cup grated Parmesan cheese
8 ounces dried bucatini pasta or spaghetti
3 cups thinly sliced sweet onions (2 large)
2 tablespoons butter or margarine
1 cup ricotta cheese
2 tablespoons snipped fresh basil or 2 teaspoons dried basil, crushed
¼ teaspoon black pepper
1 pound frozen cooked Italian meatballs, thawed
1½ cups shredded mozzarella cheese (6 ounces)
1 24- to 26-ounce jar purchased tomato and basil pasta sauce or marinara sauce
Snipped fresh parsley or basil (optional)

1. Grease a 10-inch springform pan. Line bottom of pan with parchment paper or foil. Grease parchment or foil; set pan aside. Or grease a 2-quart square baking dish.

PROSCIUTTO-WRAPPED
ASPARAGUS PANINI

MEATBALL
PIE

2. For pasta crust, in a small bowl stir together 2 of the eggs and the grated Parmesan cheese; set aside. In a large saucepan cook pasta according to package directions; drain. Return pasta to saucepan. Add egg mixture, tossing to coat. Press pasta mixture into bottom of prepared pan, building up sides slightly. Set aside.

3. Meanwhile, in a large skillet cook onions, covered, in hot butter over medium-low heat about 15 minutes or until tender and light brown, stirring occasionally. Uncover; increase heat to medium. Cook about 5 minutes or until onions are golden brown, stirring occasionally. Remove from heat.

4. Preheat oven to 350°F. In a small bowl stir together the remaining egg, the ricotta cheese, 2 tablespoons basil, and the pepper. Spread ricotta cheese mixture over pasta crust. Top with caramelized onions. Place springform pan on a large baking sheet. (If using a baking dish, it can go directly on the oven rack.) Bake for 15 minutes. Spoon ¾ cup of the pasta sauce over layers in pan. Sprinkle with ½ cup of the mozzarella cheese.

5. Toss meatballs with ¾ cup of the pasta sauce and ½ cup of the mozzarella cheese. Arrange meatball mixture over layers in pan, forming a mound. Top with ½ cup of the

remaining pasta sauce (reserve remaining pasta sauce and mozzarella cheese).

6. Cover pie loosely with foil. Bake for 45 to 50 minutes or until heated through. Sprinkle with remaining mozzarella cheese. Let stand, uncovered, for 15 minutes. Using parchment paper, lift pie out of pan. Using a serrated knife, cut pie into wedges. If desired, garnish with snipped fresh parsley before serving. Heat and pass remaining pasta sauce.

PER SERVING *542 cal., 29 g fat (15 g sat. fat), 157 mg chol., 1,029 mg sodium, 41 g carb., 5 g fiber, 29 g pro.*

CHICKEN POT PIE SOUP

Chicken Pot Pie Soup

PREP **35 minutes**
BAKE **10 minutes at 450°F**
MAKES **6 servings**

- ½ cup chopped carrot
- ½ cup chopped celery
- ⅓ cup chopped onion
- 2 cloves garlic, minced
- 1 tablespoon butter
- 4 cups chicken broth
- 2 cups chopped cooked chicken breast
- 2 cups dried medium egg noodles
- ½ teaspoon seasoned salt
- ½ teaspoon dry mustard
- ½ teaspoon chili powder
- ½ teaspoon black pepper
- ¼ teaspoon curry powder
- 1 cup half-and-half or light cream
- 1 tablespoon all-purpose flour
- 1 cup chopped fresh broccoli
- ⅓ cup frozen peas
- 1 recipe Biscuits

1. In a large saucepan cook carrot, celery, onion, and garlic in hot butter about 5 minutes or until tender. Stir in broth, chicken, noodles, and seasonings. Bring to boiling; reduce heat. Simmer, covered, 10 minutes or until noodles are tender.
2. In a bowl whisk together half-and-half and flour; add to saucepan. Add broccoli and peas. Simmer, uncovered, 5 minutes or until slightly thickened. Spoon into bowls; top with Biscuits.
Biscuits Preheat oven to 450°F. In a bowl combine 2 cups all-purpose flour, 4 teaspoons baking powder, 4 teaspoons sugar, and ½ teaspoon cream of tartar. Cut in ½ cup butter to make coarse crumbs. Make a well in center; add ⅔ cup milk. Using a fork, stir just until moistened. On a lightly floured surface gently knead dough until it holds together. Pat into an 8-inch square. Cut into 12 rectangles; place 1 inch apart on an ungreased baking sheet. Bake 10 to 12 minutes or until golden.
PER SERVING *544 cal., 26 g fat (15 g sat. fat), 117 mg chol., 1,272 mg sodium, 54 g carb., 3 g fiber, 25 g pro.*

Harvest Slaw

START TO FINISH **30 minutes**
MAKES **12 servings**

- 3 tablespoons olive oil
- 2 garlic cloves, coarsely chopped
- 2 teaspoons caraway seeds, lightly crushed
- ¼ cup cider vinegar
- 1 tablespoon honey
  Salt and black pepper
- 4 cups finely shredded red cabbage (or mix red and green)
- 2 red apples, cored and thinly sliced
- ½ cup dried cranberries
- ½ cup pecan halves, toasted (see tip, page 25)
- 2 tablespoons cilantro leaves

1. In a large skillet heat olive oil over medium heat. Add garlic and caraway seeds and cook and stir 1 minute. Whisk in the vinegar and honey and bring to a simmer to combine. Season with salt and pepper.
2. In a large bowl toss together the cabbage, apples, cranberries, and pecans. Add dressing and toss to combine. Top with cilantro.
PER SERVING *108 cal., 7 g fat (1 g sat. fat), 0 g chol., 56 mg sodium, 13 g carb., 2 g fiber, 1 g pro.*

Beet, Blue Cheese, and Almond Salad

PREP **25 minutes** COOK **20 minutes**
COOL **1 hour** MAKES **6 servings**

- 7 medium beets (2½ pounds)
- 1 small clove garlic
  Kosher salt
- 3 tablespoons extra virgin olive oil
- 2 tablespoons lemon juice
- ¾ teaspoon black pepper
- 8 ounces creamy blue cheese
- 2 ounces Marcona almonds, toasted (see tip, page 25)
- 1 tablespoon chopped fresh parsley

1. Trim and peel the beets. Cut 6 of the beets into bite-size pieces. Place in a steamer rack over a pot of boiling water. Cover the pot and steam 20 to 25 minutes, until tender.
2. Coarsely grate the remaining beet; place in a large bowl. For dressing, mash the garlic with a pinch of salt to make a paste; add to grated beet along with the oil, lemon juice, 1 teaspoon salt, and black pepper. When beets are cooked, toss them with the dressing. Cool to room temperature.
3. Crumble blue cheese over the salad and sprinkle with almonds and parsley.
PER SERVING *333 cal., 23 g fat (8 g sat. fat), 28 mg chol., 1,005 mg sodium, 21 g carb., 6 g fiber, 13 g pro.*

PEPPERED PEAR
SCONES WITH PEAR
CONSERVE

Peppered Pear Scones with Pear Conserve

PREP 25 minutes
BAKE 10 minutes at 375°F
MAKES 16 servings

1¾ cups all-purpose flour
⅓ cup packed brown sugar
2 teaspoons baking powder
½ teaspoon whole black peppercorns, cracked
¼ teaspoon baking soda
¼ teaspoon salt
⅓ cup butter
2 eggs
¼ cup grated Parmesan cheese (1 ounce)
¼ cup buttermilk
½ cup chopped, peeled fresh pear, patted dry with paper towels
Whole black peppercorns, cracked (optional)
1 cup Pear Conserve (optional)

1. Preheat oven to 375°F. In a large bowl stir together flour, brown sugar, baking powder, pepper, baking soda, and salt. Using a pastry blender, cut in butter until mixture resembles coarse crumbs. Make a well in the center of the flour mixture.
2. In a small bowl beat eggs lightly; stir in cheese and buttermilk. Add the buttermilk mixture all at once to the flour mixture. Using a fork, stir just until moistened. Fold in pear.
3. Turn out dough onto a floured surface. Quickly knead dough by folding and gently pressing for 10 to 12 strokes or until nearly smooth. Pat the dough into an 8-inch square. Cut into 16 squares.
4. Place scones 1 inch apart on an ungreased baking sheet. If desired, sprinkle with additional cracked pepper. Bake for 10 to 12 minutes or until golden. Cool on the baking sheet for 5 minutes. Transfer scones to a wire rack. Serve warm. If desired, serve with Pear Conserve.

PER SERVING 167 cal., 5 g fat (3 g sat. fat), 38 mg chol., 164 mg sodium, 28 g carb., 1 g fiber, 3 g pro.

Pear Conserve In a large saucepan combine 2½ cups chopped, peeled fresh pears; ½ cup water; and 3 tablespoons lemon juice. Bring to boiling; reduce heat. Simmer, covered, for 10 minutes. Stir in one 1.75-ounce package regular powdered fruit pectin. Bring to a full rolling boil, stirring constantly. Stir 1¾ cups sugar and ½ cup golden raisins. Return to a full rolling boil. Boil hard for 1 minute, stirring constantly. Remove from heat; if desired, stir in ⅓ cup chopped toasted pecans or walnuts (see tip, page 25), and ¼ teaspoon ground cinnamon or mace. Cool slightly.

Apple-Brandy Pies

(photo page 148)

PREP 30 minutes
BAKE 35 minutes at 375°F
COOL 25 minutes
MAKES 12 servings

1 recipe Toasted Pecan Pastry
3 cups chopped, peeled cooking apples
¼ cup brandy or lemon juice
½ cup sugar
4 teaspoons all-purpose flour
½ teaspoon apple pie spice
  Milk
1 recipe Brandy Whipped Cream (optional)
  Apple pie spice (optional)

1. Preheat oven to 375°F. Prepare Toasted Pecan Pastry. On a lightly floured surface roll pastry until ⅛ inch thick. Using a 4- to 4½-inch round cutter, cut out pastry to make 12 circles total, rerolling scraps as necessary. Gently press dough circles onto the bottoms and up the sides of 12 ungreased 2½-inch muffin cups. Using a fluted pastry wheel or a pizza cutter, cut about forty 2½×¼-inch strips from the remaining pastry, rerolling scraps as necessary; set aside.
2. For filling, in a medium bowl combine apples and brandy. In a small bowl stir together sugar, flour, and apple pie spice. Sprinkle sugar mixture over apple mixture; toss gently to coat. Spoon filling evenly into pastry-lined muffin cups. Lay 3 or 4 strips of pastry over filling in each cup, creating different patterns with the strips. Trim strips as necessary. Brush pastry strips lightly with milk.
3. Bake about 35 minutes or until pastry is golden and filling is bubbly. Cool in muffin cups on a wire rack for 5 minutes. Carefully remove pies from muffin cups; cool on wire rack about 20 minutes to serve warm or cool pies completely. If desired, serve with Brandy Whipped Cream and sprinkle with apple pie spice.

Toasted Pecan Pastry In a medium bowl stir together 1½ cups all-purpose flour, ⅓ cup very finely chopped toasted pecans, and ¼ teaspoon salt. Using a pastry blender, cut in ⅓ cup shortening and ¼ cup butter, cut up, or shortening until pieces are pea size. Sprinkle 1 tablespoon ice water over part of the flour mixture; toss gently with a fork. Push moistened pastry to one side of bowl. Repeat moistening flour mixture, using 1 tablespoon ice water at a time, until all of the flour mixture is moistened (¼ to ⅓ cup ice water total). Gather flour mixture into a ball, kneading gently until it holds together.
PER SERVING 224 cal., 12 g fat (4 g sat. fat), 10 mg chol., 77 mg sodium, 25 g carb., 1 g fiber, 2 g pro.

Brandy Whipped Cream In a chilled small mixing bowl combine ½ cup whipping cream and 1 tablespoon brandy or 1 teaspoon vanilla. Beat with the chilled beaters of an electric mixer on medium to high until stiff peaks form (tips stand straight).

Chocolate Stack Loaf

PREP 40 minutes
BAKE 14 minutes at 350°F
COOL 10 minutes
MAKES 12 servings

1 cup unbleached all-purpose flour
1 cup packed brown sugar
⅓ cup natural unsweetened cocoa powder
½ teaspoon baking soda
¼ teaspoon salt
½ cup unsalted butter, melted
2 eggs
½ teaspoon vanilla extract
½ cup hot tap water
1 recipe Easy Fudge Frosting
  Unsweetened cocoa powder

1. Position rack in lower third of oven. Preheat oven to 350°F. Lightly grease sides of 13×9×2-inch baking pan. Line bottom of pan with parchment paper.
2. In large mixing bowl whisk together flour, brown sugar, ⅓ cup cocoa powder, baking soda, and salt. Add butter, eggs, and vanilla. Whisk gently until dry ingredients are moistened and mixture resembles a thick paste. Whisk briskly about 30 strokes. Tap any batter from whisk. Use rubber spatula to stir in the hot water, scraping sides as necessary, just until batter is blended and smooth. With spatula, scrape batter from bowl into pan and spread to make a thin even layer.
3. Bake 14 to 16 minutes or until a wooden pick inserted into center comes out clean. Cool in pan on wire rack 10 minutes. Slide a thin metal spatula or knife around cake edges to loosen from pan. Invert cake onto rack. Remove paper liner; carefully turn cake right side up. Cool completely.
4. Cut cake crosswise into three equal rectangles. Thickly spread Easy Fudge Frosting on one piece, top with a second piece, and spread with frosting. Leave top unfrosted. Thickly frost long sides. Before serving, dust top with cocoa powder.

Easy Fudge Frosting In a medium saucepan melt 6 tablespoons unsalted butter; stir in cup 1 cup sugar, 1 cup unsweetened cocoa powder, and a pinch of salt. Gradually stir in 1 cup whipping cream. Heat, stirring constantly, until smooth and hot but not boiling. Remove from heat; stir in 1 teaspoon vanilla. Cool until thickened and spreadable.
PER SERVING 396 cal., 23 g fat (14 g sat. fat), 98 mg chol., 182 mg sodium, 49 g carb., 4 g fiber, 5 g pro.

CHOCOLATE
STACK LOAF